The 20th Century at the Met

# TheMetropolitanOpera®
## 2000

Universe

Equinox, solstice, and full moon dates
are given according to Eastern Standard
Time or Eastern Daylight Saving Time
as applicable.

Published by
UNIVERSE PUBLISHING
A Division of Rizzoli
International Publications, Inc.
300 Park Avenue South
New York, NY 10010

Printed in Malaysia

Front cover (clockwise from top):
Geraldine Farrar in *Madama Butterfly*
(Opera News), Tito Gobbi and Maria
Callas in *Tosca* (Metropolitan Opera
Archives), Birgit Nilsson in *Elektra*
(© Beth Bergman 1999), *The Voyage*
(© Beth Bergman 1999), Enrico Caruso
and Emmy Destinn in *La Fanciulla del
West* (*Opera News*), Leontyne Price in
*Aida* (© Beth Bergman 1999)

Back cover (clockwise from top left):
The Old Metropolitan Opera House,
Sherrill Milnes and Plácido Domingo
in *Otello* (© Beth Bergman 1999),
Giocomo Lauri-Volpi and Maria Jeritza
in *Turandot* (Metropolitan Opera
Archives), Simon Estes and Grace
Bumbry in *Porgy and Bess* (Metropolitan
Opera Guild), Luciano Pavarotti and
Joan Sutherland in *La Fille du Régiment*
(Metropolitan Opera Guild)

At the beginning of the twentieth century, the Metropolitan Opera had been in existence for nearly eighteen years. The 1900–01 season featured the United States premieres of Puccini's *La Bohème* and *Tosca*, and the Met debuts of Louise Homer and Marcel Journet. Among the other artists on the roster that year were Johanna Gadski, Lillian Nordica, Nellie Melba, Milka Ternina, David Bispham, Giuseppe Campanari, Edouard de Reszke, Antonio Pini-Corsi, Pol Plançon and Antonio Scotti. It was the final Met season for the great tenor Jean de Reszke, who with Lillian Nordica led the cast in a legendary New Year's Eve performance of *Lohengrin* that had been scheduled to usher in the new century. An orchestra ticket to the Met cost $5, while the average price for a quart of milk was $.07 and a one pound round steak cost about $.14.

The dawning of the next century is a fine time to explore the one preceding it; if we know where we've come from, we may have a better understanding of where we're going. The changes that took place at the Met over the last one hundred years are as varied and drastic as those experienced everywhere else, and the photos and captions in this calendar are an attempt to mark those changes. Only a fraction of the thousands of performances, personalities and events that have enriched Met history could be included in fifty-three pages. Some were chosen because of their importance to Met history, others to give a taste of an era.

As always, I am indebted to the Met's archives director, Robert Tuggle, whose knowledge of Met history and photographs is second to none. I would also like to thank the assistant archivist, John Pennino, for his help.


Paul Gruber
Editor

# December 1999/January

| | |
|---|---|
| Monday | 27 |

1901: NELLIE MELBA
AND THE DE RESZKE
BROTHERS IN *FAUST*

The 1900–01 season was
Maurice Grau's eighth as
general manager of the
Metropolitan Opera
House. (Four of these had
been in partnership with
Henry E. Abbey, who had
died, and John B. Schoef-
fel, who had become less
involved in the running of
the company.) Under
Grau's administration the
Met began producing
operas in their original languages (prior to that there
were Italian-only years and
German-only years), and a
number of great interna-
tional stars made their
debuts, including Emma
Eames, Lillian Nordica,
Pol Plançon, Fernando de
Lucia, Francesco Tamagno,
Victor Maurel, Johanna
Gadski and Antonio Scotti.
Foremost among the voices
of this golden age were the
Australian soprano Nellie
Melba and the Polish
brothers, tenor Jean de
Reszke and bass Edouard
de Reszke, shown in this
guache by T. de Thulstrup
taking their curtain calls
following a performance of
Gounod's *Faust*, as they
did on January 4, 1901.

Painting courtesy of the
Metropolitan Opera Archives.
Photograph by D. James Dee

| | |
|---|---|
| Tuesday | 28 |

FRANCESCO TAMAGNO, 1850.

GERALDINE FARRAR SHARES THE MET STAGE WITH A FLOCK OF
GEESE IN THE WORLD PREMIERE OF *KÖNIGSKINDER* IN 1910.

| | |
|---|---|
| Wednesday | 29 |

| | |
|---|---|
| Thursday | 30 |

JUNE ANDERSON, 1952.

| | |
|---|---|
| Friday | 31 |

| | | | |
|---|---|---|---|
| Saturday | 1 | Sunday | 2 |

NEW YEAR'S DAY

GUSTAV MAHLER MAKES HIS MET DEBUT AS
CONDUCTOR OF *TRISTAN AND ISOLDE*, 1908.

TEXACO-MET BROADCAST: *THE GREAT GATSBY*

TITO SCHIPA, 1888.
MICHAEL TIPPETT, 1905.

## January

| S | M | T | W | T | F | S |
|---|---|---|---|---|---|---|
| | | | | | | 1 |
| 2 | 3 | 4 | 5 | 6 | 7 | 8 |
| 9 | 10 | 11 | 12 | 13 | 14 | 15 |
| 16 | 17 | 18 | 19 | 20 | 21 | 22 |
| 23 | 24 | 25 | 26 | 27 | 28 | 29 |
| 30 | 31 | | | | | |

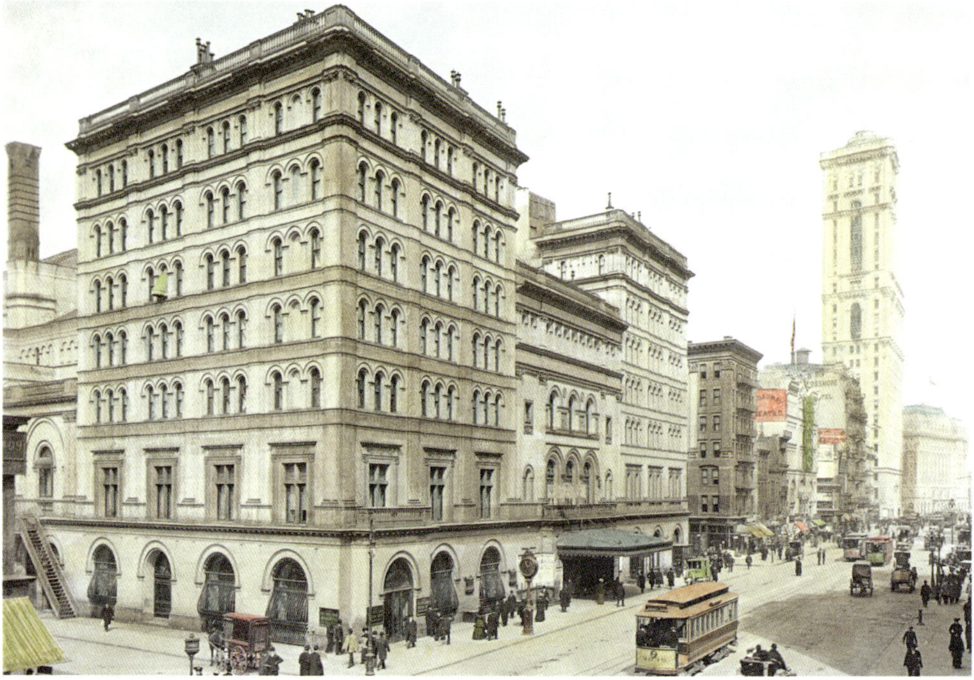

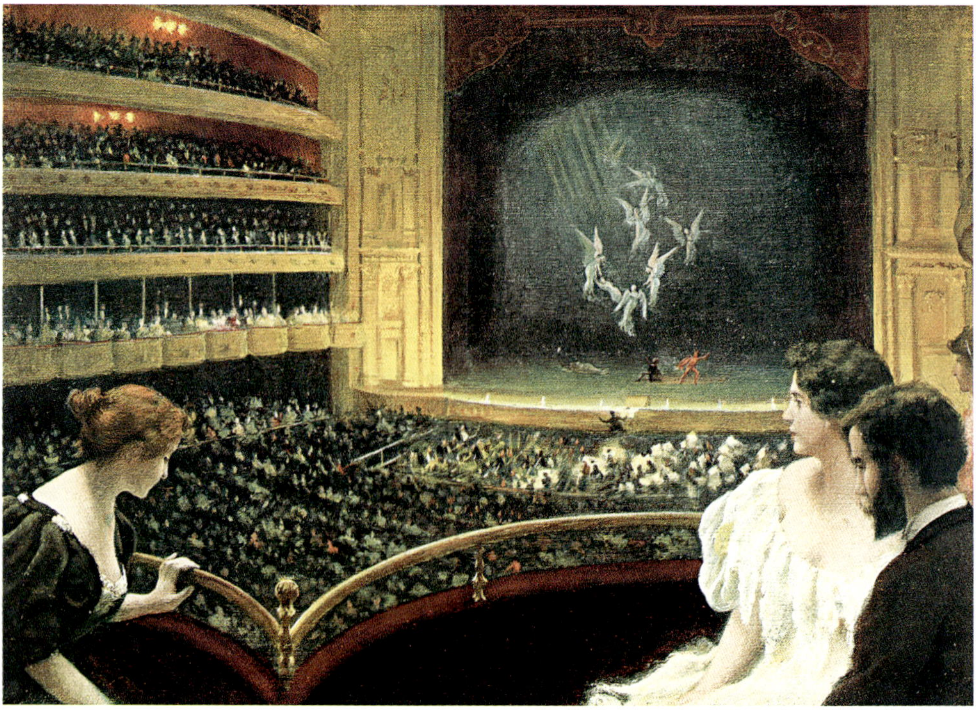

## 1900: OUTSIDE AND INSIDE THE OLD MET

When the Met first opened on Broadway between 39th and 40th Streets, the theater district was centered about five blocks south on Herald Square; only one other theater was as far north, the Casino on 39th Street, which had opened the year before the Met. But by the turn of the century, Joshua Cleaveland Cady's "yellow brick brewery" was surrounded by three more legitimate theaters, and what we now think of as the Broadway theater district began to take form. Seen to the right is the Times Tower, built a few blocks north of the Met in 1905 and which, although resurfaced, is still standing. (After its completion, what had been called Longacre Square become known as Times Square.) Below is a painting by C.C. Curran showing a Met audience enjoying, once again, *Faust*. The proscenium arch shown is the one that enclosed the stage between the fire of 1892 and a renovation of the house in 1903.

Photographs courtesy of *Opera News*

| February | | | | | | |
|---|---|---|---|---|---|---|
| S | M | T | W | T | F | S |
| | | 1 | 2 | 3 | 4 | 5 |
| 6 | 7 | 8 | 9 | 10 | 11 | 12 |
| 13 | 14 | 15 | 16 | 17 | 18 | 19 |
| 20 | 21 | 22 | 23 | 24 | 25 | 26 |
| 27 | 28 | 29 | | | | |

Monday **3**

HENRIETTE SONTAG, 1806.
LILY PONS MAKES HER MET DEBUT AS LUCIA, 1931.

Tuesday **4**

GRACE BUMBRY, 1937.
THE MET PRESENTS THE U.S. PREMIERE OF WAGNER'S *DIE MEISTERSINGER*, 1886.

Wednesday **5**

ALEXANDER KIPNIS MAKES HIS MET DEBUT IN A MATINEE *PARSIFAL*, 1940,
AND JARMILA NOVOTNÁ BOWS THE SAME EVENING AS MIMÌ.

Thursday **6**

MAFALDA FAVERO, 1905.

Friday **7**

FRANCIS POULENC, 1899.
JOHN BROWNLEE, 1901.

Saturday **8**

GIORGIO TOZZI, 1923.
EVELYN LEAR, 1926.

TEXACO-MET BROADCAST: *TOSCA*

Sunday **9**

JACQUES URLUS, 1867.
RUDOLF BING, 1902.
WALTRAUD MEIER, 1956.

# January

Monday                                                    10

SHERRILL MILNES, 1935.
JAMES MORRIS, 1947.

Tuesday                                                   11

LOTTE LEHMANN MAKES HER MET DEBUT AS SIEGLINDE, 1934.

Wednesday                                                 12

THEODOR UPPMAN, 1920.

Thursday                                                  13

RENATO BRUSON, 1936.
LEONARD WARREN MAKES HIS MET DEBUT IN *SIMON BOCCANEGRA*, 1939.

Friday                                                    14

JEAN DE RESZKE, 1850.
BEN HEPPNER, 1956.

Saturday                    15        Sunday              16

THE MET PRESENTS THE WORLD PREMIERE
OF BARBER'S *VANESSA*, 1958.
                                      PILAR LORENGAR, 1928.
TEXACO-MET BROADCAST: *RIGOLETTO*     MARILYN HORNE, 1934.

---

**1903: *PARSIFAL* BREAKS OUT OF BAYREUTH**

Following Grau's retirement in 1903, Heinrich Conreid became general manager. Less than a month after his first opening night, Conreid created controversy by staging the first performance of Wagner's *Parsifal* to be seen outside of Bayreuth. (The late composer had dictated that the work never be performed anywhere but in his Festival theater and his surviving family had tried, unsuccessfully, to block the Met production in court.) Critics and audiences took to Wagner's final music drama, and twelve performances sold out at premium prices. This cartoon from a German-language, American newspaper spoofed the production, suggesting that a cakewalk might be inserted into the sacred work.

Cartoon courtesy of *Opera News*

| February | | | | | | |
|---|---|---|---|---|---|---|
| S | M | T | W | T | F | S |
| | | | 1 | 2 | 3 | 4 | 5 |
| 6 | 7 | 8 | 9 | 10 | 11 | 12 |
| 13 | 14 | 15 | 16 | 17 | 18 | 19 |
| 20 | 21 | 22 | 23 | 24 | 25 | 26 |
| 27 | 28 | 29 | | | | |

John Martinazzi.
Handle With Care.
Metropolitan Opera Company

DISTRUCTION — APRIL 18, 1906

# January

## 1906: THE MET ON TOUR

From its first season the Met toured its productions (the 1883 tour included stops in Boston, Brooklyn, Philadelphia, Chicago, St. Louis, Cincinnati, Washington and Baltimore). On horse-drawn carts like the one shown above, the company would haul instruments, sets, costumes and props, and even a trip to Brooklyn was time consuming. The Met's greatest touring adventure took place in San Francisco on the night of April 17, 1906, when, after a performance of *Carmen* the famous earthquake struck. While there were no company fatalities, the Met lost more than $200,000 in sets and costumes, and had to give another $118,000 in refunds for performances that did not take place. Many of the company members lost personal possessions in the earthquake and fire; seen here arriving in Chicago after surviving the earthquake are Nathan Franko, Edyth Walker, Robert Blass, Marcella Sembrich, Bella Alten, Ernest Goerlitz and Enrico Caruso.

Photographs courtesy of *Opera News*

### February

| S | M | T | W | T | F | S |
|---|---|---|---|---|---|---|
|   |   | 1 | 2 | 3 | 4 | 5 |
| 6 | 7 | 8 | 9 | 10 | 11 | 12 |
| 13 | 14 | 15 | 16 | 17 | 18 | 19 |
| 20 | 21 | 22 | 23 | 24 | 25 | 26 |
| 27 | 28 | 29 |   |   |   |   |

---

Monday 17

MARTIN LUTHER KING, JR. DAY (US)
JON VICKERS MAKES HIS MET DEBUT IN *PAGLIACCI*, 1960.

Tuesday 18

KATIA RICCIARELLI, 1946.

Wednesday 19

HANS HOTTER, 1909.
TITTA RUFFO MAKES HIS MET DEBUT IN *IL BARBIERE DI SIVIGLIA*, 1922.

Thursday 20

FULL MOON

Friday 21

PLÁCIDO DOMINGO, 1941.

Saturday 22

ROSA PONSELLE, 1897.
THE 1907 U.S. PREMIERE OF STRAUSS' *SALOME* CREATES A SCANDAL, AND THE OPERA IS NOT SEEN AT THE MET AGAIN UNTIL 1934.

TEXACO-MET BROADCAST: *CAVALLERIA RUSTICANA/PAGLIACCI*

Sunday 23

TERESA ZYLIS-GARA, 1935.

# January

24

FARINELLI, 1705.

Tuesday

25

ANTONIO SCOTTI, 1866.
WILHELM FURTWÄNGLER, 1886.
RICHARD TUCKER MAKES HIS MET DEBUT IN *LA GIOCONDA*. 1945.

Wednesday

26

Thursday

27

WOLFGANG AMADEUS MOZART, 1756.
DOUBLE DEBUT OF LEONTYNE PRICE AND FRANCO CORELLI. *IL TROVATORE*. 1961.

Friday

28

MARIE CORNÉLIE FALCON, 1814.

Saturday

29

Sunday

30

JUSTINO DÍAZ, 1940.
FREDERICK DELIUS, 1862.

TEXACO-MET BROADCAST:
*DER ROSENKAVALIER*

WALTER DAMROSCH, 1862.

1907: OLIVE FREMSTAD IN *SALOME*

No stranger to controversy, Conreid managed to alienate the Met board of directors that controlled the opera house with his production of Richard Strauss's *Salome* in 1907. The work had not yet been seen in this country, and knowing that many would find it offensive both in its music and its subject matter, Conreid scheduled an open dress rehearsal on a Sunday morning, which many would attend immediately following church services. The premiere took place the following week, and critic Henry Krehbiel was not alone in feeling that "there is not a whiff of fresh and healthy air blowing through *Salome* . . ." J.P. Morgan summoned his board the next morning, and they canceled all future performances of the work. *Salome* was not seen again at the Met until 1934.

Photograph courtesy of *Opera News*

## February

| S | M | T | W | T | F | S |
|---|---|---|---|---|---|---|
| | | 1 | 2 | 3 | 4 | 5 |
| 6 | 7 | 8 | 9 | 10 | 11 | 12 |
| 13 | 14 | 15 | 16 | 17 | 18 | 19 |
| 20 | 21 | 22 | 23 | 24 | 25 | 26 |
| 27 | 28 | 29 | | | | |

1907: GERALDINE FARRAR IN *MADAMA BUTTERFLY*

In 1907 Conreid convinced Puccini to come to New York for the first time for a festival of his works, including the Met's first *Madama Butterfly* (the staging of which Puccini "supervised"), performances of *La Bohème* and the American premiere of *Manon Lescaut.* The Met's first Cio-Cio San and Pinkerton were the American soprano Geraldine Farrar and the legendary Enrico Caruso, the latter having made his Met debut four years earlier. Puccini was far from happy with their performances: he wrote his publisher, Tito Ricordi, that "Farrar . . . sings out of tune and forces, and her voice doesn't carry well in the large space," and told another friend that Caruso "won't learn anything; he's lazy and he's too pleased with himself." The public disagreed, and Farrar eventually sang 137 Met performances of the role, more than any other soprano.

Photograph courtesy of *Opera News*

| February | | | | | | |
|---|---|---|---|---|---|---|
| S | M | T | W | T | F | S |
| | | 1 | 2 | 3 | 4 | 5 |
| 6 | 7 | 8 | 9 | 10 | 11 | 12 |
| 13 | 14 | 15 | 16 | 17 | 18 | 19 |
| 20 | 21 | 22 | 23 | 24 | 25 | 26 |
| 27 | 28 | 29 | | | | |

Monday 31

PHILIP GLASS, 1937
RENATA TEBALDI MAKES HER MET DEBUT AS DESDEMONA, 1955.

Tuesday 1

CLARA BUTT, 1872.
GERMAINE LUBIN, 1890.
RENATA TEBALDI, 1922.
CAROL NEBLETT, 1946.

Wednesday 2

LISA DELLA CASA, 1919.
MARTINA ARROYO, 1936.
KIRSTEN FLAGSTAD MAKES HER MET DEBUT AS SIEGLINDE, 1935.

Thursday 3

GIULIO GATTI-CASAZZA, 1869.
CLAIRE WATSON, 1927.
HELGA DERNESCH, 1939.

Friday 4

ERICH LEINSDORF, 1912.
MARTTI TALVELA, 1935.
THE MET PRESENTS THE U.S. PREMIERES OF *FALSTAFF* IN 1895 AND *TOSCA* IN 1901.

Saturday 5

JUSSI BJOERLING, 1911.
OTTO EDELMANN, 1917.
LEONIE RYSANEK MAKES HER MET DEBUT IN *MACBETH*, 1959.

TEXACO-MET BROADCAST: *LA TRAVIATA*

Sunday 6

FIRST TEAMING OF FLAGSTAD AND MELCHIOR AS ISOLDE AND TRISTAN, 1935.

# February

## Monday 7

CLAUDIA MUZIO, 1889.

## Tuesday 8

NATHANIEL MERRILL, 1927.
ELLY AMELING, 1934.

## Wednesday 9

ALBAN BERG, 1885.
HILDEGARD BEHRENS, 1937.
LICIA ALBANESE DEBUTS IN *MADAMA BUTTERFLY*, 1940,
AND KIRI TE KANAWA DEBUTS AS DESDEMONA, 1974.

## Thursday 10

MARIA CEBOTARI, 1910.
CESARE SIEPI, 1923.
LEONTYNE PRICE, 1927.

## Friday 11

## Saturday 12

ANNY KONETZNI, 1902.
FRANCO ZEFFIRELLI, 1923.

TEXACO-MET BROADCAST:
*LES CONTES D'HOFFMANN*

## Sunday 13

FEODOR CHALIAPIN, 1873.
ALEXANDER KIPNIS, 1891.
EILEEN FARRELL, 1920.
BIDU SAYÃO MAKES HER DEBUT AS
MANON, 1937.

---

1908: *PUCK* MAGAZINE COVER

The New York press took great interest in the events of the opera world, and in November 1908 the cover of *Puck* satirized the rivalry between the Metropolitan Opera and Oscar Hammerstein's Manhattan Opera, whose intendants are shown throwing singers at each other. Giulio Gatti-Casazza had only recently been made the Met's general manager (he had been the director of La Scala for ten years), and one of his first problems was Hammerstein, who had a knack for presenting new operas and singers before the Met was able to get them. Two years later, the Met's president Otto Kahn took care of the problem by buying Hammerstein out of business for a fee of $1,200,000.

Photograph courtesy of
*Opera News*

| March | | | | | | |
|---|---|---|---|---|---|---|
| S | M | T | W | T | F | S |
| | | 1 | 2 | 3 | 4 | |
| 5 | 6 | 7 | 8 | 9 | 10 | 11 |
| 12 | 13 | 14 | 15 | 16 | 17 | 18 |
| 19 | 20 | 21 | 22 | 23 | 24 | 25 |
| 26 | 27 | 28 | 29 | 30 | 31 | |

VOL. LXIV. No. 1654.　　　PUCK BUILDING, New York, November 11th, 1908.　　　PRICE TEN CENTS.

"What Fools these Mortals be!"

# Puck

　　　Entered at N. Y. P. O. as Second-class Mail Matter.

GRAND OPERA OPENS.

1910: EMMY DESTINN AND ENRICO CARUSO IN *LA FANCIULLA DEL WEST*

When Puccini was visiting New York he was urged to see a new play by David Belasco, one of the authors of the play *Madame Butterfly*. He was not immediately enthusiastic about *Girl of the Golden West*, but his interest grew after reading the play in Italian translation, and he liked the idea of writing a wild West opera. In 1908 Gatti-Casazza and his artistic director Arturo Toscanini secured the rights to the world premiere of the work, which was completed two years later. Directed by Belasco, the starry cast included Caruso as the bandit Ramerrez (aka Dick Johnson), the great Czech soprano Emmy Destinn as Minnie and Pasquale Amato as Jack Rance. The premiere was conducted by Toscanini. This time Puccini was happy with the Met production, and on his way home he wrote to a friend, "Caruso great, Amato excellent, Toscanini, immense and good, a real angel."

Photograph courtesy of *Opera News*

### March

| S | M | T | W | T | F | S |
|---|---|---|---|---|---|---|
|   |   |   | 1 | 2 | 3 | 4 |
| 5 | 6 | 7 | 8 | 9 | 10 | 11 |
| 12 | 13 | 14 | 15 | 16 | 17 | 18 |
| 19 | 20 | 21 | 22 | 23 | 24 | 25 |
| 26 | 27 | 28 | 29 | 30 | 31 |   |

Monday    14

VALENTINE'S DAY

THE MET PRESENTS THE U.S. PREMIERE OF STRAVINSKY'S *THE RAKE'S PROGRESS*, 1953.

Tuesday    15

MARCELLA SEMBRICH, 1858.
HINA SPANI, 1896.

Wednesday    16

GERAINT EVANS, 1922.

Thursday    17

MARIAN ANDERSON, 1897.
MARJORIE LAWRENCE, 1909.

Friday    18

RITA GORR, 1926.

Saturday    19

FULL MOON

ADELINA PATTI, 1843.
JEAN-PIERRE PONNELLE, 1932.

TEXACO-MET BROADCAST: *MEFISTOFELE*

Sunday    20

MARY GARDEN, 1874.
NADINE CONNER, 1913.

# February

## Monday 21

LÉO DELIBES, 1836.

## Tuesday 22

GIOVANNI ZENATELLO, 1876.

## Wednesday 23

GEORGE FRIDERIC HANDEL, 1685.

## Thursday 24

ARRIGO BOITO, 1842.
RENATA SCOTTO, 1934.

## Friday 25

## Saturday 26

EMMY DESTINN, 1878.

TEXACO-MET BROADCAST:
*MADAMA BUTTERFLY*

## Sunday 27

MATTIA BATTISTINI, 1856.
ENRICO CARUSO, 1873.
LOTTE LEHMANN, 1888.
MIRELLA FRENI, 1935.

---

### 1915: TOSCANINI, FARRAR AND GATTI

This is one of the great candid Met photographs. Gatti-Casazza, Toscanini and Farrar are on the set of Giordano's opera *Madame Sans-Gêne,* and Gatti holds his head in woe as he listens to his prima donna. It's possible they were discussing the weather, but given that Farrar and Toscanini had been romantically involved for half a decade and that she had demanded he leave his family for her, it's likely that the discussion was not congenial. A few months after the photo was taken Toscanini resigned and returned to Italy.

Photograph courtesy of *Opera News*

---

### March

| S | M | T | W | T | F | S |
|---|---|---|---|---|---|---|
|   |   |   | 1 | 2 | 3 | 4 |
| 5 | 6 | 7 | 8 | 9 | 10 | 11 |
| 12 | 13 | 14 | 15 | 16 | 17 | 18 |
| 19 | 20 | 21 | 22 | 23 | 24 | 25 |
| 26 | 27 | 28 | 29 | 30 | 31 |   |

1916: GIOVANNI
MARTINELLI IN
*GOYESCAS*

In 1912, Gatti-Casazza
heard a young tenor in
Italy and signed him to a
Met contract for the
1913–14 season. Giovanni
Martinelli made his
debut for the company as
Rodolfo in 1913, and his
career with the Met did
not end until 1946—926
performances later. (No
leading tenor has ever sung
more Met performances,
and no leading tenor is
ever likely to.) Two of his
first roles were in world
premieres: Lefebvre in
*Madame Sans-Gêne* and Fernando in Enrique Grana-
dos's *Goyescas*. The latter,
which played but five
performances in 1916,
was a stage adaptation of
Granados's piano suite of
the same name, based on
Goya's paintings. The composer and his wife came to
New York for the premiere
and were on their way
home to Europe on the
*S.S. Sussex* when the ship
was torpedoed by the Ger-
mans; neither survived.

Photograph courtesy of
*Opera News*

| | March | | | | | |
|---|---|---|---|---|---|---|
| S | M | T | W | T | F | S |
| | | | 1 | 2 | 3 | 4 |
| 5 | 6 | 7 | 8 | 9 | 10 | 11 |
| 12 | 13 | 14 | 15 | 16 | 17 | 18 |
| 19 | 20 | 21 | 22 | 23 | 24 | 25 |
| 26 | 27 | 28 | 29 | 30 | 31 | |

**Monday 28**

MARIO ANCONA, 1860.
GERALDINE FARRAR, 1882.

**Tuesday 29**

**Wednesday 1**

DIMITRI MITROPOULOS, 1896.
LUCINE AMARA, 1925.

**Thursday 2**

BEDŘICH SMETANA, 1824.
KURT WEILL, 1900.
SIMON ESTES, 1938.

**Friday 3**

ROBERTA ALEXANDER, 1949.
MARILYN HORNE MAKES HER MET DEBUT IN *NORMA*, 1970.

**Saturday 4**

ANTONIO VIVALDI, 1678.
BERNARD HAITINK, 1929.
LEONARD WARREN DIES ON THE MET STAGE
DURING A PERFORMANCE
OF *LA FORZA DEL DESTINO*, 1960.

TEXACO-MET BROADCAST:
*THE MERRY WIDOW*

**Sunday 5**

ALESSIO DE PAOLIS, 1893.

# March

Monday · 6

GINA CIGNA, 1900.
JULIUS RUDEL, 1921.
NORMAN TREIGLE, 1927.
KIRI TE KANAWA, 1944.

Tuesday · 7

MAURICE RAVEL, 1875.

Wednesday · 8

ASH WEDNESDAY

INTERNATIONAL WOMEN'S DAY

RUGGERO LEONCAVALLO, 1857.

Thursday · 9

SAMUEL BARBER, 1910.
THOMAS SCHIPPERS, 1930.

Friday · 10

LORENZO DA PONTE, 1749.
MARIA BARRIENTOS, 1884.
EVA TURNER, 1892.

Saturday · 11

TEXACO-MET BROADCAST: *LA CENERENTOLA*

Sunday · 12

HANS KNAPPERTSBUSCH, 1888

---

1918: ENRICO CARUSO, ROSA PONSELLE AND JOSÉ MARDONES IN *LA FORZA DEL DESTINO*

Met history is rich with sensational debuts, but the most extraordinary may well have been that of Rosa Ponselle. Having sung only in vaudeville and movie theaters, churches and cafés (usually with her sister Carmela), Ponselle auditioned for Gatti-Casazza and Caruso; a mere six months later she was given the leading role in the Met premiere of a major work by Verdi, joining a cast that included Caruso, Giuseppe De Luca and José Mardones. Critics judged her a great talent who had much to learn, and as Robert Tuggle points out, she was not to achieve the promise of her debut "until *La Vestale*, seven years later, when, her magnificent natural voice under perfect control, the Ponselle people remember and what she made of herself became the same."

Photograph courtesy of *Opera News*

April

| S | M | T | W | T | F | S |
|---|---|---|---|---|---|---|
|  |  |  |  |  |  | 1 |
| 2 | 3 | 4 | 5 | 6 | 7 | 8 |
| 9 | 10 | 11 | 12 | 13 | 14 | 15 |
| 16 | 17 | 18 | 19 | 20 | 21 | 22 |
| 23 | 24 | 25 | 26 | 27 | 28 | 29 |
| 30 |  |  |  |  |  |  |

1919/1920: JOSEPH
URBAN DESIGNS FOR
*LA JUIVE* AND *DON
CARLO*

In an effort to improve
production values,
Gatti-Casazza brought in
several new scenic designers, but none had a more
lasting impact on the look
of Met productions than
Joseph Urban. Born in
Vienna, Urban enjoyed a
long Broadway career that
was launched when his
work was seen by Florenz
Ziegfeld. The designer
created the sets for all the
*Ziegfeld Follies* from 1915
to 1931, as well as other
important shows including
*Show Boat*. (He was also
the architect of the
Ziegfeld Theater.) Gatti
brought him in to design
sets and costumes for a
new *Faust* in 1917, the
first of fifty-four Met productions to bear his unique
design and color sense.
Some were still being used
as late as 1962, and sixteen
had costumes by Urban's
daughter Gretel. Seen here
are his renderings for *La
Juive* (1919) and *Don Carlo*
(1920).

Renderings courtesy of
*Opera News*

| April | | | | | | |
|---|---|---|---|---|---|---|
| S | M | T | W | T | F | S |
| | | | | | | 1 |
| 2 | 3 | 4 | 5 | 6 | 7 | 8 |
| 9 | 10 | 11 | 12 | 13 | 14 | 15 |
| 16 | 17 | 18 | 19 | 20 | 21 | 22 |
| 23 | 24 | 25 | 26 | 27 | 28 | 29 |
| 30 | | | | | | |

Monday 13

FRITZ BUSCH, 1890.
ROSALIND ELIAS, 1930.

Tuesday 14

OLIVE FREMSTAD, 1871.

Wednesday 15

ROSA PAULY, 1894.
ANTONIETTA STELLA, 1929.

Thursday 16

CHRISTA LUDWIG, 1924.
TERESA BERGANZA, 1934.
ROGER NORRINGTON, 1934.

Friday 17

ST. PATRICK'S DAY
VICTORIA DE LOS ANGELES MAKES HER DEBUT AS MARGUERITE, 1951.

Saturday 18

Sunday 19

NIKOLAI RIMSKY-KORSAKOV, 1844

TEXACO-MET BROADCAST:
*LADY MACBETH OF MTSENSK*

FULL MOON

THE MET PRESENTS THE U.S. PREMIERE OF
MUSSORGSKY'S *BORIS GODUNOV*, 1913.

# March

Monday    20

FIRST DAY OF SPRING

BENIAMINO GIGLI, 1890.
LAURITZ MELCHIOR, 1890.

Tuesday    21

JOHANN SEBASTIAN BACH, 1685.
MODEST MUSSORGSKY, 1839.
PASQUALE AMATO, 1878.

Wednesday    22

EMMANUEL LIST, 1886.
MARTHA MÖDL, 1912.

Thursday    23

RÉGINE CRESPIN, 1927.
NORMAN BAILEY, 1933.

Friday    24

MARIA MALIBRAN, 1808.
DOLORA ZAJICK, 1952.

Saturday    25

ARTURO TOSCANINI, 1867.
BÉLA BARTÓK, 1881.
MAGDA OLIVERO, 1912.

TEXACO-MET BROADCAST: *DAS RHEINGOLD*

Sunday    26

PIERRE BOULEZ, 1925.

---

**1922: FEODOR CHALIAPIN IN *DON CARLO***

One of the supreme artists of the century, Feodor Chaliapin had two Met careers. While still a member of the Bolshoi theater, the bass came to the Met in 1907, making his debut as Boito's Mefistofele and also singing Gounod's Méphistophélès, Basilio in *Il Barbiere di Siviglia* and Leporello. His performances were controversial; his acting was more naturalistic than that usually seen in the opera house, and many were shocked when he appeared half-naked as Mefistofele. Several of the more influential New York critics wrote scathing reviews of his Basilio, and he left the city hoping not to return. But fourteen years later Chaliapin decided to leave Russia (the Communists had confiscated his property), and returned to the Met as Boris Godunov, which he sang in the original language while his colleagues sang in Italian. When he appeared in *Don Carlo*, the critic Pitts Sanborn wrote of his interpretation of Philip's great monologue, "Other basses have sung this air, some of them extremely well; Chaliapin lived it."

Photograph courtesy of
*Opera News*

| | | | April | | | |
|---|---|---|---|---|---|---|
| S | M | T | W | T | F | S |
| | | | | | | 1 |
| 2 | 3 | 4 | 5 | 6 | 7 | 8 |
| 9 | 10 | 11 | 12 | 13 | 14 | 15 |
| 16 | 17 | 18 | 19 | 20 | 21 | 22 |
| 23 | 24 | 25 | 26 | 27 | 28 | 29 |
| 30 | | | | | | |

## 1923: BENIAMINO GIGLI IN *L'AFRICANA*

After Caruso left the Met in 1920, it took two great tenors to replace him: Giovanni Martinelli and Beniamino Gigli. (Many would argue that five hundred tenors could not have replaced him.) Gigli's first Met performance—as Boito's Faust—took place less than a month before Caruso's last, and the *Times* review was modestly enthusiastic: ". . . he sings not without finish and style. . . . He will no doubt be another valuable accession to the company." Gigli's sweet, expressive voice earned him a legion of fans and made him the most popular lyric tenor of his day. Aside from Rodolfo, his most frequent Met role was Vasco da Gama in Meyerbeer's *L'Africana* (as the opera was known in its Italian translation), and his first performance was with Rosa Ponselle and Adamo Didur. Gigli sang thirteen Met seasons, a stay that would have been longer had he not had a falling out with the company over Depression-era pay cuts.

Photograph courtesy of *Opera News*

|   | April |   |   |   |   |   |
|---|---|---|---|---|---|---|
| S | M | T | W | T | F | S |
|   |   |   |   |   |   | 1 |
| 2 | 3 | 4 | 5 | 6 | 7 | 8 |
| 9 | 10 | 11 | 12 | 13 | 14 | 15 |
| 16 | 17 | 18 | 19 | 20 | 21 | 22 |
| 23 | 24 | 25 | 26 | 27 | 28 | 29 |
| 30 |   |   |   |   |   |   |

Monday **27**

MARIA EWING, 1950.

Tuesday **28**

ANTONIO TAMBURINI, 1800.
SAMUEL RAMEY, 1942.

Wednesday **29**

WILLIAM WALTON, 1902

Thursday **30**

Friday **31**

FRANZ JOSEPH HAYDN, 1732.
ELISABETH GRÜMMER, 1911.

Saturday **1**

RENATO ZANELLI, 1892.
GÜNTHER RENNERT, 1911.

TEXACO-MET BROADCAST: *DIE WALKÜRE*

Sunday **2**

KURT HERBERT ADLER, 1905.

# April

## Monday 3

JORMA HYNNINEN, 1941.

## Tuesday 4

PIERRE MONTEUX, 1875.
JANE EAGLEN, 1960.

## Wednesday 5

HERBERT VON KARAJAN, 1908.

## Thursday 6

## Friday 7

GIOVANNI BATTISTA RUBINI, 1794.
BEVERLY SILLS MAKES HER MET DEBUT IN *L'ASSEDIO DI CORINTO*, 1975.

## Saturday 8

JOSEF KRIPS, 1902.
WALTER BERRY, 1929.

TEXACO-MET BROADCAST:
*PELLÉAS ET MÉLISANDE*

## Sunday 9

JULIUS PATZAK, 1898.
ANTAL DORATI, 1906.
CLOE ELMO, 1910.

---

1926: GIOCOMO LAURI-VOLPI AND MARIA JERITZA IN *TURANDOT*

Those critics who complained about the spectacle of the 1987 Franco Zeffirelli Met production of *Turandot* might have done well to read about the American premiere of Puccini's opera, presented by the company in 1926. According to the *New York Times*, the onstage personnel included "120 opera chorus, 120 chorus school, 60 boy choir singers, 60 ballet girls, 30 male dancers and procession leaders, 30 stage musicians, 230 extra 'supers'—650 persons, all told, besides the 11-star cast and a hundred orchestra players in the pit." That eleven-star cast was led by the tempestuous Czech soprano Maria Jeritza, who had made a somewhat belated Met debut five years earlier, and the Italian tenor Giacomo Lauri-Volpi. At first hearing, Olin Downes of the *Times* was disappointed with the opera and asked, "Where is invention, humanity, passion in all this music? . . . The score relies more and more upon the stage and the situations to carry it through—Much ado, musically speaking, about almost nothing."

Photograph courtesy of the Metropolitan Opera Archives

### May

| S | M | T | W | T | F | S |
|---|---|---|---|---|---|---|
|  | 1 | 2 | 3 | 4 | 5 | 6 |
| 7 | 8 | 9 | 10 | 11 | 12 | 13 |
| 14 | 15 | 16 | 17 | 18 | 19 | 20 |
| 21 | 22 | 23 | 24 | 25 | 26 | 27 |
| 28 | 29 | 30 | 31 |  |  |  |

# April

## 1931: THE MET TAKES TO THE AIR

On December 25, 1931, an important tradition was established: weekly radio broadcasts from the Met stage. Some very early attempts of radio transmission had been made in 1910 (including a *Tosca* with Fremstad and a *Pagliacci* with Caruso and Amato), but the Christmas day *Hänsel und Gretel* was the first performance covered by an agreement between the Met and NBC, which provided for two seasons of twenty-four broadcasts each. Editha Fleischer and Queena Mario (shown here) played the title roles, and the program was carried by more than one hundred stations and short-waved abroad. For the first season, composer and critic Deems Taylor annoyed listeners by providing commentary spoken over the music, but this innovation was not retained. In 1940, sponsorship of the broadcasts was taken over by the Texas Company—now known as Texaco—an extraordinary relationship that continues to the present day.

Photograph courtesy of *Opera News*

### May

| S | M | T | W | T | F | S |
|---|---|---|---|---|---|---|
|   | 1 | 2 | 3 | 4 | 5 | 6 |
| 7 | 8 | 9 | 10 | 11 | 12 | 13 |
| 14 | 15 | 16 | 17 | 18 | 19 | 20 |
| 21 | 22 | 23 | 24 | 25 | 26 | 27 |
| 28 | 29 | 30 | 31 |   |   |   |

### Monday 10

LUIGI ALVA, 1927.
ORGANIZATIONAL MEETING OF THE METROPOLITAN OPERA COMPANY TAKES PLACE, 1880.

### Tuesday 11

KURT MOLL, 1938.

### Wednesday 12

LILY PONS, 1898.
MONTSERRAT CABALLÉ, 1933.

### Thursday 13

MARGARET PRICE, 1941.

### Friday 14

GEORGE CEHANOVSKY, 1892.
SALVATORE BACCALONI, 1900.
APRILE MILLO, 1958.

### Saturday 15

MARGARETE OBER, 1885.
NEVILLE MARRINER, 1924.

TEXACO-MET BROADCAST: *SIEGFRIED*

### Sunday 16

PALM SUNDAY

MARIE COLLIER, 1926.
GALA FAREWELL TO THE OLD MET, 1966.

# April

Monday                                                    17

SIEGFRIED JERUSALEM, 1940.
THE METROPOLITAN OPERA COMPANY SURVIVES THE SAN FRANCISCO EARTHQUAKE AND
FIRE WHILE ON TOUR, 1906.

Tuesday                                                   18

FULL MOON

LEOPOLD STOKOWSKI, 1882.
FRIDA LEIDER, 1888.
GEORGE SHIRLEY, 1934.
CATHERINE MALFITANO, 1948.

Wednesday                                                 19

Thursday                                                  20

PASSOVER

JOHN ELIOT GARDINER, 1943.

Friday                                                    21

GOOD FRIDAY

LEONARD WARREN, 1911.

Saturday                22          Sunday                23

KATHLEEN FERRIER, 1912.
FIORENZA COSSOTTO, 1935.
GALA FAREWELL TO RUDOLF BING, 1972.

TEXACO-MET BROADCAST:                   EASTER
GÖTTERDÄMMERUNG                         SERGEI PROKOFIEV, 1891.

1933: LAWRENCE
TIBBETT IN *THE
EMPEROR JONES*

No Met general manager
presented more new operas
than Gatti-Casazza; of the
twenty-nine world
premieres produced at the
Met through 1999, twenty-
one occurred during Gatti's
tenure. Many of these were
given but a few perfor-
mances and became foot-
notes in Met history, but
one of the more successful
was Louis Gruenberg's
1933 *The Emperor Jones*,
based on Eugene O'Neill's
1920 play. The premiere
had been scheduled to take
place in Berlin but was
canceled in fear that the
Nazi government would
not smile on a work about
a black American. Baritone
Lawrence Tibbett was
therefore given a chance to
shine in the title role,
albeit in blackface, and it
was largely due to Tibbett's
performance and populari-
ty as a singer that the
opera was given fifteen
times over two seasons.

Photograph courtesy of
*Opera News*

|   | May |   |   |   |   |   |
|---|---|---|---|---|---|---|
| S | M | T | W | T | F | S |
|   | 1 | 2 | 3 | 4 | 5 | 6 |
| 7 | 8 | 9 | 10 | 11 | 12 | 13 |
| 14 | 15 | 16 | 17 | 18 | 19 | 20 |
| 21 | 22 | 23 | 24 | 25 | 26 | 27 |
| 28 | 29 | 30 | 31 |   |   |   |

# April

## 1935: METROPOLITAN OPERA SURPRISE PARTIES

For four seasons, from 1932 to 1935, the Met staged an annual event called the "Grand Operatic Surprise Party," a gala performance in which stars of the Met and guests often performed unexpected turns. The final such performance took place on March 31, 1935, and included appearances by nearly every star on the Met roster. They were joined by Beatrice Lillie, who clowned her way through the first act of *Carmen* in several languages (singing "chez mon ami Lilli Palmer" and asking her Don José—Paul Althouse, dressed as Siegfried—"Parlez-vous Francez? Do yuz?"). Shown here are Lily Pons and Lauritz Melchior, who as acrobats did a number called "Allez-Oop."

Photograph courtesy of the Metropolitan Opera Archives

| Monday | 24 |
|---|---|

| Tuesday | 25 |
|---|---|

ASTRID VARNAY, 1918.

| Wednesday | 26 |
|---|---|

FLORENCE AUSTRAL, 1894.
WILMA LIPP, 1925.

| Thursday | 27 |
|---|---|

FRIEDRICH VON FLOTOW, 1812.
JUDITH BLEGEN, 1941.

| Friday | 28 |
|---|---|

FRANCIS ROBINSON, 1910.
JEFFREY TATE, 1943.

| Saturday | 29 | Sunday | 30 |
|---|---|---|---|

THOMAS BEECHAM, 1879.
ZUBIN MEHTA, 1936.

FRANZ LEHÁR, 1870.
LOUISE HOMER, 1871.

### May

| S | M | T | W | T | F | S |
|---|---|---|---|---|---|---|
| | 1 | 2 | 3 | 4 | 5 | 6 |
| 7 | 8 | 9 | 10 | 11 | 12 | 13 |
| 14 | 15 | 16 | 17 | 18 | 19 | 20 |
| 21 | 22 | 23 | 24 | 25 | 26 | 27 |
| 28 | 29 | 30 | 31 | | | |

# May

Monday                                                               1

MAY DAY BANK HOLIDAY (UK)

Tuesday                                                              2

MICHAEL BOHNEN, 1887.
JEANNINE ALTMEYER, 1948.

Wednesday                                                           3

MAX ALVARY, 1856.
LÉOPOLD SIMONEAU, 1918.

Thursday                                                            4

ROBERTA PETERS, 1930.

Friday                                                              5

MARIA CANIGLIA, 1905.

Saturday                        6     Sunday                        7

GHENA DIMITROVA, 1941.                PETER ILYICH TCHAIKOVSKY, 1840.
                                      ELISABETH SÖDERSTRÖM, 1927.

---

### 1935: LAURITZ MELCHIOR AND KIRSTEN FLAGSTAD IN *TRISTAN AND ISOLDE*

Four days after making a sensational Met debut as Sieglinde, Kirsten Flagstad was back onstage as Isolde for the first of her seventy-three Met performances in the role. All but seven of these were with an artist most would consider the greatest heldentenor of the twentieth century, Lauritz Melchior, who managed to sing 128 performances as Tristan in his twenty-four-season Met career. Perhaps Melchior's heroic Tristan was already being taken for granted—he had been singing the role for the company since 1929—but the lion's share of critical praise went to Flagstad, as when Lawrence Gilman wrote in the *New York Herald Tribune* "Last night's performance . . . was made unforgettable for its hearers by a transcendently beautiful and moving impersonation of Isolde—an embodiment as sensitively musical, so fine-grained in its imaginative and intellectual texture, so lofty in its pathos and simplicity, of so memorable a loveliness, that experienced opera-goers sought among their memories of legendary days to find its like."

Photograph courtesy of the Metropolitan Opera Archives

| | | | June | | | |
|---|---|---|---|---|---|---|
| S | M | T | W | T | F | S |
| | | | | | 1 | 2 | 3 |
| 4 | 5 | 6 | 7 | 8 | 9 | 10 |
| 11 | 12 | 13 | 14 | 15 | 16 | 17 |
| 18 | 19 | 20 | 21 | 22 | 23 | 24 |
| 25 | 26 | 27 | 28 | 29 | 30 | |

# May

## 1942: LICIA ALBANESE IN *LA TRAVIATA*

Succeeding Gatti-Casazza as general manager was tenor Edward Johnson, who would see the company through the rest of the Depression as well as through the war years. The war affected the Met's supply of singers in several ways: some European artists who came over just before the war stayed, while the stranding of others in Europe gave a number of important American singers the chance to shine. Among the former was Licia Albanese, who had been recommended to Johnson by Beniamino Gigli, with whom she had recorded *La Bohème* in Italy in 1939. Albanese had two signature roles: Cio-Cio-San, with which she made her Met debut in 1940, and Violetta, for which critic Virgil Thomson awarded her a figurative "royal crown" in "the coronation of stardom." Arturo Toscanini agreed and cast her in the role for his famous 1946 NBC broadcast of *La Traviata*; at eighty-seven performances, Albanese still holds the Met record for appearances in the role.

Photograph courtesy of *Opera News*

| | | June | | | | |
|---|---|---|---|---|---|---|
| S | M | T | W | T | F | S |
| | | | | | 1 | 2 | 3 |
| 4 | 5 | 6 | 7 | 8 | 9 | 10 |
| 11 | 12 | 13 | 14 | 15 | 16 | 17 |
| 18 | 19 | 20 | 21 | 22 | 23 | 24 |
| 25 | 26 | 27 | 28 | 29 | 30 | |

**Monday 8**

HEATHER HARPER, 1930.
CARLO COSSUTTA, 1932.
FELICITY LOTT, 1947.

**Tuesday 9**

CARLO MARIA GIULINI, 1914.
ANNE SOFIE VON OTTER, 1955.
GROUNDBREAKING FOR THE NEW MET AT LINCOLN CENTER, 1963.

**Wednesday 10**

ANGELICA CATALINI, 1780.
JOSEF SVOBODA, 1920.

**Thursday 11**

ALMA GLUCK, 1884.
BIDÚ SAYÃO, 1902.

**Friday 12**

JULES MASSENET, 1842.
LILLIAN NORDICA, 1857.
MARIANO STABILE, 1888.
GIULIETTA SIMIONATO, 1910.

**Saturday 13**

ARTHUR SULLIVAN, 1842.

**Sunday 14**

MOTHER'S DAY

OTTO KLEMPERER, 1885.
PATRICE MUNSEL, 1925.

# May

## Monday 15

CLAUDIO MONTEVERDI, 1567.
FIRST METROPOLITAN OPERA "AUDITIONS OF THE AIR" TAKE PLACE, 1937.

## Tuesday 16

RICHARD TAUBER, 1891.
JAN KIEPURA, 1902.

## Wednesday 17

FAUSTO CLEVA, 1902.
ZINKA MILANOV, 1906.
BIRGIT NILSSON, 1918.
GABRIEL BACQUIER, 1924.

## Thursday 18

FULL MOON

EZIO PINZA, 1892.
BORIS CHRISTOFF, 1914.

## Friday 19

NELLIE MELBA, 1861.
KERSTIN THORBORG, 1896.
THE MET EMBARKS ON ITS FIRST TOUR ABROAD, TAKING SIX OPERAS TO PARIS, 1910.

## Saturday 20

## Sunday 21

---

1943: JAMES MELTON, ZINKA MILANOV, BIDÙ SAYÃO, JARMILA NOVOTNÁ AND EZIO PINZA IN *DON GIOVANNI*

The Met enjoyed a Mozart renaissance in the forties, sparked largely by the availability of Bruno Walter to conduct and Ezio Pinza to play roles like Figaro, Sarastro and Don Giovanni. Pinza's Giovanni, which he first sang at the Met in 1929, took on new depth after his Salzburg performances with Walter in the late thirties. The Met surrounded him with extraordinary colleagues; seen with him in this 1943 revival are James Melton as Don Ottavio, Zinka Milanov as Donna Anna, Bidù Sayão as Zerlina and Jarmila Novotná as Donna Elvira.

Photograph courtesy of *Opera News*

## 1949: LJUBA WELITSCH IN *SALOME*

On February 4, 1949, a meteor hit the Met stage in the form of Ljuba Welitsch, making her debut as Salome. (Also making his first appearance with the company that night was conductor Fritz Reiner.) The Bulgarian soprano had already sung the role in a number of European theaters (including Covent Garden, where she starred in a controversial production staged by Peter Brook, with sets by Salvador Dali). But the New York audience was astonished by the ease with which she rode above Reiner's orchestra, as well as the raw theatricality of her acting. (At her curtain call she was greeted with a fifteen-minute ovation, which is long even by operatic standards.) Welitsch's "go-for-broke" vocalism was to take its toll fairly quickly, but those who heard her Salome in 1949 were unlikely to forget it.

Photograph courtesy of the Metropolitan Opera Archives

Monday

22

VICTORIA DAY (CANADA)

RICHARD WAGNER, 1813.
JAMES KING, 1925.

Tuesday

23

ROSA RAISA, 1893.

Wednesday

24

JOAN HAMMOND, 1912.

Thursday

25

BEVERLY SILLS, 1929.

Friday

26

INGE BORKH, 1917.
TERESA STRATAS, 1938.

Saturday

27

Sunday

28

JACQUES HALÉVY, 1799.
LINA PAGLIUGHI, 1907.

DIETRICH FISCHER-DIESKAU, 1925.
ELENA SOULIOTIS, 1943.

### June

| S | M | T | W | T | F | S |
|---|---|---|---|---|---|---|
|   |   |   |   |   | 1 | 2 | 3 |
| 4 | 5 | 6 | 7 | 8 | 9 | 10 |
| 11 | 12 | 13 | 14 | 15 | 16 | 17 |
| 18 | 19 | 20 | 21 | 22 | 23 | 24 |
| 25 | 26 | 27 | 28 | 29 | 30 |   |

# May/June

1949: DOROTHY
KIRSTEN IN *MANON
LESCAUT*

Puccini's first successful
opera had been absent
from the Met stage for
twenty seasons when it was
presented in a new production—made possible by a
gift from the Metropolitan
Opera Guild—on Novem-
ber 23, 1949. The critics
had high praise for both
the work and the artists
singing the leading roles,
Dorothy Kirsten and Jussi
Bjoerling. Of Kirsten, who
had made her Met debut
four years earlier, Olin
Downes wrote in the *New
York Times* "Dorothy
Kirsten . . . sang her solo
delightfully, and then, in
the duet with Des Grieux,
sang with a degree of emo-
tion and sweep of line that
she had not achieved
before in our experience."
After singing the role for a
number of years, Kirsten
told *Opera News* that she
thought the opera would
be more theatrical if
Puccini had ended it after
the third act, calling the
fourth act "a letdown."

Photograph courtesy of
*Opera News*

Monday                                29

MEMORIAL DAY (US)
SPRING BANK HOLIDAY (UK)

MET BEGINS ITS FIRST TOUR OF JAPAN, 1975.

Tuesday                               30

GEORGE LONDON, 1920.

Wednesday                             31

FRANCES ALDA, 1883.
SHIRLEY VERRETT, 1931.

Thursday                               1

MARGARETE MATZENAUER, 1881.
SIGRID ONÉGIN, 1889.
FREDERICA VON STADE, 1945.

Friday                                 2

EDWARD ELGAR, 1857.
NEIL SHICOFF, 1949.

Saturday            3     Sunday       4

JAN PEERCE, 1904.

ROBERT MERRILL, 1917.
FEDORA BARBIERI, 1920.
CECILIA BARTOLI, 1966.

| | | | June | | | |
|---|---|---|---|---|---|---|
| S | M | T | W | T | F | S |
| | | | | 1 | 2 | 3 |
| 4 | 5 | 6 | 7 | 8 | 9 | 10 |
| 11 | 12 | 13 | 14 | 15 | 16 | 17 |
| 18 | 19 | 20 | 21 | 22 | 23 | 24 |
| 25 | 26 | 27 | 28 | 29 | 30 | |

# June

## 1950: JUSSI BJOERLING AND DELIA RIGAL IN *DON CARLO*

When the Met's new general manager, Rudolf Bing, presented his first opening night in 1950, he broke with tradition in several ways. The opera chosen was Verdi's *Don Carlo*, now recognized as a masterwork, but at the time of Bing's first season unheard for nearly thirty years. Hoping to strengthen the quality of productions, Bing turned to the theater for directors and designers, choosing the Shakespearean director Margaret Webster to stage *Don Carlo*. (She was also the first woman to direct for the Met stage.) This rare photo taken from the wings shows Jussi Bjoerling and Delia Rigal as Don Carlo and Elisabeth; on opening night, they were joined by Robert Merrill, Fedora Barbieri, Cesare Siepi and Jerome Hines, with Fritz Stiedry conducting.

Photograph courtesy of the Metropolitan Opera Archives

**Monday** 5

JAMES LEVINE MAKES HIS MET DEBUT CONDUCTING *TOSCA*. 1971.

**Tuesday** 6

KLAUS TENNSTEDT, 1926.
GIACOMO ARAGALL, 1939.

**Wednesday** 7

GEORGE SZELL, 1897.
ANDREA VELIS, 1932.
ROBERTO ALAGNA, 1963.

**Thursday** 8

RAYMOND MICHALSKI, 1930.

**Friday** 9

OTTO NICOLAI, 1810.
TITTA RUFFO, 1877.
ILEANA COTRUBAS, 1939.

**Saturday** 10

HARICLEA DARCLÉE, 1860.

**Sunday** 11

RICHARD STRAUSS, 1864.
RISÉ STEVENS, 1913.

# June

## Monday 12

POL PLANÇON, 1851.
VANNI-MARCOUX, 1877.

## Tuesday 13

ELISABETH SCHUMANN, 1885.

## Wednesday 14

JOHN MCCORMACK, 1884.
RUDOLF KEMPE, 1910.

## Thursday 15

ERNESTINE SCHUMANN-HEINK, 1861.
JOHANNA GADSKI, 1872.

## Friday 16

FULL MOON

JERRY HADLEY, 1952.

## Saturday 17

CHARLES GOUNOD, 1818.
VICTOR MAUREL, 1848.
IGOR STRAVINSKY, 1882.
MIGNON DUNN, 1931.

## Sunday 18

FATHER'S DAY

EVA MARTON, 1943.

---

1951: ELEANOR STEBER, BLANCHE THEBOM AND PATRICE MUNSEL IN *COSÌ FAN TUTTE*

In his second season Bing hired the actor and director Alfred Lunt to stage Mozart's *Così Fan Tutte*, another great opera that had been out of the Met repertory for many years. Lunt created an elegant and seamless ensemble with a cast almost entirely American-born: Eleanor Steber, Blanche Thebom, Patrice Munsel, Richard Tucker, Frank Guerrara and John Brownlee (the latter from Australia). The production was sung in an English translation by Ruth and Thomas Martin, and for the first season Lunt began the proceedings by appearing as a footman, lighting candles, pausing for latecomers to be seated and giving Fritz Stiedry the cue to begin the overture.

Photograph courtesy of the Metropolitan Opera Archives

## 1952: RISË STEVENS IN *CARMEN*

Risë Stevens was already the Met's preeminent Carmen when Bing hired Tyrone Guthrie to direct a new production in 1952, but she agreed to restudy the role with Guthrie and conductor Fritz Reiner, and her new interpretation was more successful than ever. One of Guthrie's major innovations was to set most of the fourth act in Escamillo's dressing room, rather than in the square outside the bull ring. This was primarily for budgetary reasons, but Guthrie theorized that Carmen was less likely to escape Don José's knife if she were trapped inside the room with him, and with his leading lady the director devised a harrowing death scene in which she clutched a window curtain, pulling it down with her as she fell.

Photograph courtesy of the Metropolitan Opera Archives

**Monday**

19

ANNELIESE ROTHENBERGER, 1924.

**Tuesday**

20

FIRST DAY OF SUMMER

JACQUES OFFENBACH, 1819.

**Wednesday**

21

**Thursday**

22

JENNIE TOUREL, 1900.
PETER PEARS, 1910.

**Friday**

23

JAMES LEVINE, 1943.

**Saturday**

24

**Sunday**

25

GUSTAVE CHARPENTIER, 1860.
FIRST "MET IN THE PARKS" PERFORMANCE
IS *LA BOHÈME*, 1967.

July

| S | M | T | W | T | F | S |
|---|---|---|---|---|---|---|
| | | | | | | 1 |
| 2 | 3 | 4 | 5 | 6 | 7 | 8 |
| 9 | 10 | 11 | 12 | 13 | 14 | 15 |
| 16 | 17 | 18 | 19 | 20 | 21 | 22 |
| 23 | 24 | 25 | 26 | 27 | 28 | 29 |
| 30 | 31 | | | | | |

# June/July

**Monday** 26

FRIEDA HEMPEL, 1885.
WOLFGANG WINDGASSEN, 1914.
GIUSEPPE TADDEI, 1916.
CLAUDIO ABBADO, 1933.

**Tuesday** 27

TOTI DAL MONTE, 1893.
ANNA MOFFO, 1932.

**Wednesday** 28

THOMAS HAMPSON, 1955.

**Thursday** 29

LUISA TETRAZZINI, 1871.
RAFAEL KUBELIK, 1914.

**Friday** 30

**Saturday** 1

**Sunday** 2

PETER ANDERS, 1908.
THE METROPOLITAN OPERA GUILD IS
FOUNDED BY MRS. AUGUST BELMONT, 1935.

CHRISTOPH WILLIBALD VON GLUCK, 1714.

1952/1963: EUGENE BERMAN DESIGNS FOR *LA FORZA DEL DESTINO* AND *OTELLO*

Bing's quest for improved production values at the Met extended to design as well as staging, and one of the fine artists he brought to the company was the Russian-born Eugene Berman. Beginning with *Rigoletto* in 1951, Berman created sets and costumes for five Met productions, the others being *La Forza del Destino* (1952—shown above), *Il Barbiere di Siviglia* (1954), *Don Giovanni* (1957) and *Otello* (1963—shown below). Berman's painterly designs were stageworthy enough to serve the Met for years, with *Forza* and *Don Giovanni* being used as late as 1984.

Renderings courtesy of *Opera News*

| | | | July | | | |
|---|---|---|---|---|---|---|
| S | M | T | W | T | F | S |
| | | | | | | 1 |
| 2 | 3 | 4 | 5 | 6 | 7 | 8 |
| 9 | 10 | 11 | 12 | 13 | 14 | 15 |
| 16 | 17 | 18 | 19 | 20 | 21 | 22 |
| 23 | 24 | 25 | 26 | 27 | 28 | 29 |
| 30 | 31 | | | | | |

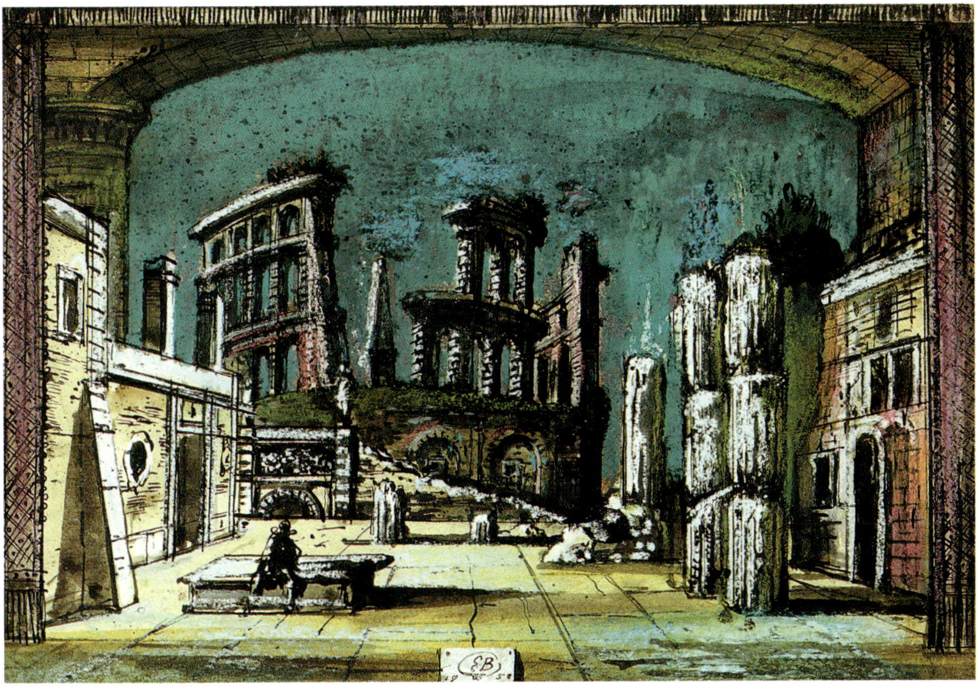

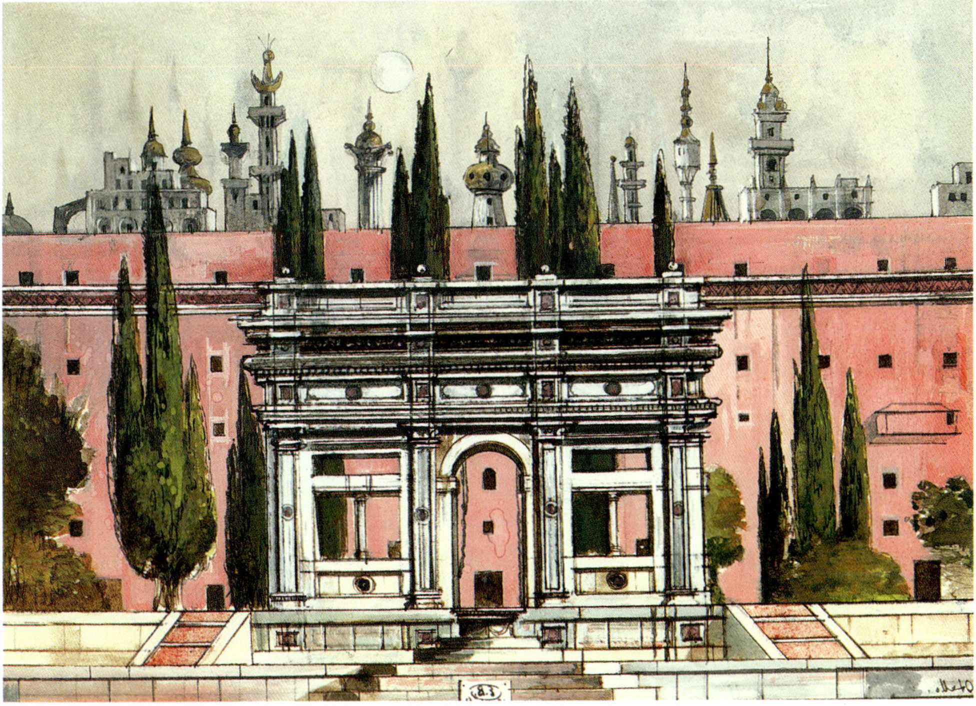

# July

## 1955: RUDOLF BING WELCOMES MARIAN ANDERSON TO THE MET

In his memoirs, Rudolf Bing called Marian Anderson's Met debut as the first featured black singer in the company's history "among my proudest moments in the house." Possessing one of the great voices of the century, Anderson was primarily a recitalist; she was not an actress, and preferred working with an accompanist rather than orchestras and conductors. (In fact, she never again sang in an opera after her Met performances.) Ulrica in *Un Ballo in Maschera* was a good role for Anderson at that period in her career ("officially" fifty-two, she was actually fifty-seven at the time of her Met debut), and her eight performances at the Met were largely symbolic, used by Bing to announce to the public that as far as he was concerned, race would no longer be a consideration for casting.

Photograph courtesy of *Opera News*

**Monday** 3

CANADA DAY OBSERVED

LEOŠ JANÁČEK, 1854.
CARLOS KLEIBER, 1930.
BRIGITTE FASSBAENDER, 1939.

**Tuesday** 4

INDEPENDENCE DAY (US)

**Wednesday** 5

**Thursday** 6

DOROTHY KIRSTEN, 1910.

**Friday** 7

GUSTAV MAHLER, 1860.
GIAN CARLO MENOTTI, 1911.
ELENA OBRAZTSOVA, 1937.

**Saturday** 8

CHRISTEL GOLTZ, 1912.

**Sunday** 9

EBERHARD WÄCHTER, 1929.

### August

| S | M | T | W | T | F | S |
|---|---|---|---|---|---|---|
| | | 1 | 2 | 3 | 4 | 5 |
| 6 | 7 | 8 | 9 | 10 | 11 | 12 |
| 13 | 14 | 15 | 16 | 17 | 18 | 19 |
| 20 | 21 | 22 | 23 | 24 | 25 | 26 |
| 27 | 28 | 29 | 30 | 31 | | |

# July

Monday                                                          10

CARL ORFF, 1895.
LJUBA WELITSCH, 1913.
JOSEPHINE VEASEY, 1930.

Tuesday                                                         11

EBE STIGNANI, 1903.
NICOLAI GEDDA, 1925.
HERMANN PREY, 1929.

Wednesday                                                       12

KIRSTEN FLAGSTAD, 1895.

Thursday                                                        13

CARLO BERGONZI, 1924.

Friday                                                          14

Saturday          15          Sunday          16

CHARLES ANTHONY, 1929.          FULL MOON

## 1957: CESARE SIEPI IN *DON GIOVANNI*

Cesare Siepi has been playing Mozart's Don Juan at the Met since 1952 when he took center stage in the 1957 production by Herbert Graf and Eugene Berman, along with Eleanor Steber, Lisa Della Casa, Roberta Peters, Cesare Valletti, Fernando Corena, Theodor Uppman and Giorgio Tozzi, with conductor Karl Böhm making his Met debut. European experience had deepened Siepi's characterization, and Howard Taubman in the *New York Times* wrote "Cesare Siepi's Don Giovanni has grown in magnetism and diablerie. His voice is smoother, mellower, more supple than ever. His Champagne Aria is headier than any product of the vine, and his Serenade is sensuous enough to melt any girl's heart." Siepi's ninety-one performances in the role set the Met record.

Photograph courtesy of the Metropolitan Opera Archives

| August | | | | | | |
|---|---|---|---|---|---|---|
| S | M | T | W | T | F | S |
|  |  | 1 | 2 | 3 | 4 | 5 |
| 6 | 7 | 8 | 9 | 10 | 11 | 12 |
| 13 | 14 | 15 | 16 | 17 | 18 | 19 |
| 20 | 21 | 22 | 23 | 24 | 25 | 26 |
| 27 | 28 | 29 | 30 | 31 |  |  |

# July

## 1961: LEONTYNE PRICE IN *AIDA*

Marian Anderson broke the Met's color barrier in 1956, but it wasn't until Leontyne Price's debut in 1961 that a black artist was able to achieve a major career there. Price's debut role was Leonora in *Il Trovatore* (Franco Corelli made his debut the same evening), but her signature role was Aida, which she eventually sang forty-two times with the company. Much later, Price was to write, "I think I was born knowing Aida." The opera was chosen for her farewell Met appearance, an emotional performance that millions watched on a live telecast.

Photograph courtesy of the Metropolitan Opera Archives

**Monday 17**

THERESE TIETJENS, 1831.
HERMANN JADLOWKER, 1877.
ELEANOR STEBER, 1914.
DAWN UPSHAW, 1960.

**Tuesday 18**

PAULINE VIARDOT, 1821.
KURT MASUR, 1927.

**Wednesday 19**

DINH GILLY, 1877.
ROBERT O'HEARN, 1921.
AMY SHUARD, 1924.

**Thursday 20**

**Friday 21**

HERBERT WITHERSPOON, 1873.

**Saturday 22**

LICIA ALBANESE, 1913.

**Sunday 23**

FRANCESCO CILEA, 1866.

### August

| S | M | T | W | T | F | S |
|---|---|---|---|---|---|---|
| | | 1 | 2 | 3 | 4 | 5 |
| 6 | 7 | 8 | 9 | 10 | 11 | 12 |
| 13 | 14 | 15 | 16 | 17 | 18 | 19 |
| 20 | 21 | 22 | 23 | 24 | 25 | 26 |
| 27 | 28 | 29 | 30 | 31 | | |

# July

| Monday | 24 |

GIUSEPPE DI STEFANO, 1921.

| Tuesday | 25 |

| Wednesday | 26 |

| Thursday | 27 |

MARIO DEL MONACO, 1915.
CAROL VANESS, 1952.

| Friday | 28 |

GIUDITTA GRISI, 1805.
GIULIA GRISI, 1811.
RICCARDO MUTI, 1941.

| Saturday | 29 | Sunday | 30 |

PETER SCHREIER, 1935.

## 1965: MARIA CALLAS AND RUDOLF BING

The battles between Rudolf Bing and Maria Callas are well-known to opera-lovers—they were covered in the press in great detail and have since been written about endlessly. In 1965 the singer agreed to return to the Met after a seven-year absence for two performances of *Tosca*, and this candid backstage photo was taken of the general manager and the diva. The print shown here was given to Bing by Callas and inscribed, "To Rudolf with deep affection and sincere friendship in memory of our special performances and his affectionate care of me. Maria Callas, 1965."

Photograph courtesy of the Metropolitan Opera Archives

### August

| S | M | T | W | T | F | S |
|---|---|---|---|---|---|---|
|   |   | 1 | 2 | 3 | 4 | 5 |
| 6 | 7 | 8 | 9 | 10 | 11 | 12 |
| 13 | 14 | 15 | 16 | 17 | 18 | 19 |
| 20 | 21 | 22 | 23 | 24 | 25 | 26 |
| 27 | 28 | 29 | 30 | 31 |   |   |

To Rudolf with
deep affection and
respectful friendship:
in memory of our
performances and the
affectionate love of ours.

Maria Callas
1965

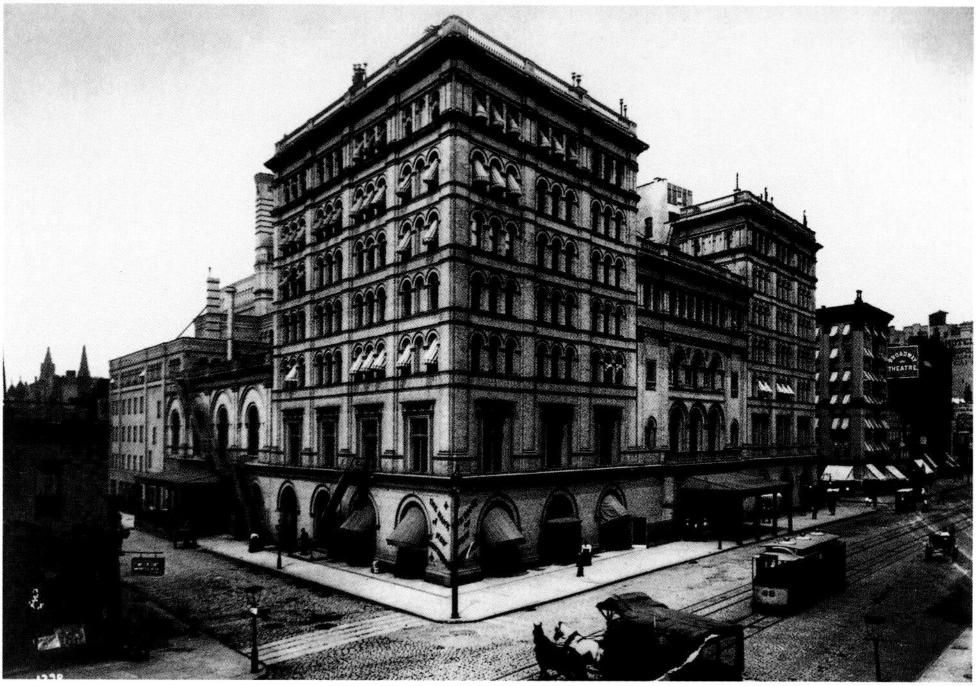
BROADWAY
THEATRE

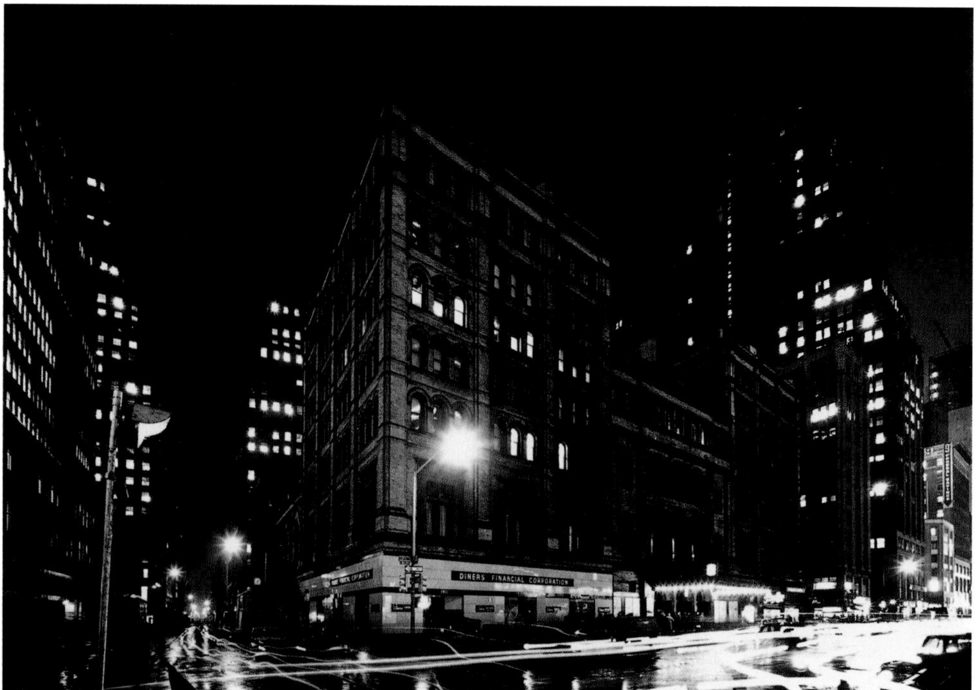
DINERS FINANCIAL CORPORATION

## 1900/1966: THE OLD MET EXTERIOR

The transformation of a city block over a sixty-six-year period can be seen in these two photographs of the old Met exterior, the first taken at the turn of the century and the second near the end of the building's existence. The entire neighborhood around the Met had changed considerably—the theater district had moved five blocks uptown, and the modest apartment houses and theaters surrounding the opera house were replaced by large office buildings. The exterior of the old Met was never judged an architectural gem and age had not improved it, except as a symbol for the art it housed.

Photographs courtesy of
*Opera News*

Monday

31

Tuesday

1

THEO ADAM, 1926.

Wednesday

2

CLAIRE DUX, 1885.
JOHN DEXTER, 1925.
GUNDULA JANOWITZ, 1937.

Thursday

3

Friday

4

FRANCO CORELLI, 1921.
JESS THOMAS, 1927.
GABRIELLA TUCCI, 1929.

### August

| S | M | T | W | T | F | S |
|---|---|---|---|---|---|---|
|   |   | 1 | 2 | 3 | 4 | 5 |
| 6 | 7 | 8 | 9 | 10 | 11 | 12 |
| 13 | 14 | 15 | 16 | 17 | 18 | 19 |
| 20 | 21 | 22 | 23 | 24 | 25 | 26 |
| 27 | 28 | 29 | 30 | 31 |   |   |

Saturday

5

Sunday

6

AMBROISE THOMAS, 1811.
ERICH KLEIBER, 1890.

# August

Monday 7

Tuesday 8

Wednesday 9

ROLF GÉRARD, 1909.

Thursday 10

Friday 11

The old Met auditorium
had been renovated several
times in its eighty-three-
year existence, but its
majesty and grandeur were
unchallenged. The back-
stage facilities of the theater, however, had long
been judged both inade-
quate and obsolete. Plans
for a new opera house had
been discussed since the
1920s (sites at Rockefeller
Center and near Columbus
Circle had been seriously
considered), but the
Depression and World War
II made the massive pro-
ject of building a new Met
impossible. In the mid-
1950s an urban renewal
project near Lincoln
Square began to take
shape, promising future
homes for not only the
Met, but the New York
Philharmonic, New York
City Opera and New York
City Ballet as well. Within
a few years it became obvi-
ous that the days of the
"yellow brick brewery"
were numbered.

Photograph courtesy of
*Opera News*

Saturday 12

Sunday 13

ETTORE PANIZZA, 1875.
MARIA OLCZEWSKA, 1892.
PETER HOFMANN, 1944.

EMMA EAMES, 1865.
KATHLEEN BATTLE, 1948.

September

| S | M | T | W | T | F | S |
|---|---|---|---|---|---|---|
|   |   |   |   |   | 1 | 2 |
| 3 | 4 | 5 | 6 | 7 | 8 | 9 |
| 10 | 11 | 12 | 13 | 14 | 15 | 16 |
| 17 | 18 | 19 | 20 | 21 | 22 | 23 |
| 24 | 25 | 26 | 27 | 28 | 29 | 30 |

## 1966: FAREWELL TO THE OLD MET— LEOPOLD STOKOWSKI AND THE AUDIENCE

Rudolf Bing had planned to close the old building with a performance of *Faust*, but the board of the Guild convinced him that nothing would do but an all-star, farewell gala, both as an emotional experience and a fund-raising opportunity. (In the end the gala raised more than $300,000.) A black-tie audience of luminaries and socialites (note Ethel Merman in the front row) enjoyed a evening long on sentiment: a group of luminaries from the past marched in to the "Entrance of the Guests" from *Tannhäuser*, and several great artists made their final Met appearances that night, including Licia Albanese, Eleanor Steber and Zinka Milanov.

Photograph courtesy of *Opera News*

**Monday** 14

MARTIAL SINGHER, 1904.
FERRUCCIO TAGLIAVINI, 1913.
GEORGES PRÊTRE, 1924.

**Tuesday** 15

FULL MOON

EMMA CALVÉ, 1858.
RITA HUNTER, 1933.

**Wednesday** 16

**Thursday** 17

**Friday** 18

GEMMA BELLINCIONI, 1864.
LEO SLEZAK, 1873.

**Saturday** 19

**Sunday** 20

CHRISTINE NILSSON, 1843.

### September

| S | M | T | W | T | F | S |
|---|---|---|---|---|---|---|
| | | | | | 1 | 2 |
| 3 | 4 | 5 | 6 | 7 | 8 | 9 |
| 10 | 11 | 12 | 13 | 14 | 15 | 16 |
| 17 | 18 | 19 | 20 | 21 | 22 | 23 |
| 24 | 25 | 26 | 27 | 28 | 29 | 30 |

# August

## Monday
### 21

JANET BAKER, 1933.

## Tuesday
### 22

CLAUDE DEBUSSY, 1862.
EDWARD JOHNSON, 1878.

## Wednesday
### 23

## Thursday
### 24

## Friday
### 25

KING LUDWIG II OF BAVARIA, 1845.
LEONARD BERNSTEIN, 1918.
JOSÉ VAN DAM, 1940.

## Saturday
### 26

GRÉ BROUWENSTIJN, 1915.
WOLFGANG SAWALLISCH, 1923.

## Sunday
### 27

FIRE SEVERELY DAMAGES THE METROPOLITAN
OPERA HOUSE, 1892, AND NECESSITATES THE
CANCELLATION OF THE FOLLOWING SEASON.

1966: FAREWELL TO
THE OLD MET—THE
FINAL CURTAIN

The final number on the
program of the Farewell
Gala was the trio finale
from *Faust*—the first
opera heard in the house—
sung by Gabriella Tucci,
Nicolai Gedda and Jerome
Hines. Following this, the
entire company gathered
onstage to sing "Auld Lang
Syne" with the audience.

Photograph courtesy of
*Opera News*

### September

| S | M | T | W | T | F | S |
|---|---|---|---|---|---|---|
|   |   |   |   |   | 1 | 2 |
| 3 | 4 | 5 | 6 | 7 | 8 | 9 |
| 10 | 11 | 12 | 13 | 14 | 15 | 16 |
| 17 | 18 | 19 | 20 | 21 | 22 | 23 |
| 24 | 25 | 26 | 27 | 28 | 29 | 30 |

# August/September

**1966: THE NEW MET UNDER CONSTRUCTION**

Although the opening of the new Metropolitan Opera House was first announced for the fall of 1961 and later for 1964, construction took much longer than expected. By August 1964, when this photograph was taken from where the stage would be, the Parterre, Grand Tier, Dress Circle and Balcony levels could be discerned beneath the five arches. The cost of the theater was originally estimated at $15 million, but the price tag eventually came to more than $49 million.

Photograph courtesy of
*Opera News*

---

Monday **28**

SUMMER BANK HOLIDAY (UK)
UMBERTO GIORDANO, 1867.
KARL BÖHM, 1894.
RICHARD TUCKER, 1913.
PAUL PLISHKA, 1941.

---

Tuesday **29**

HELGE ROSWAENGE, 1897.
THOMAS STEWART, 1928.

---

Wednesday **30**

REGINA RESNIK, 1922.

---

Thursday **31**

AMILCARE PONCHIELLI, 1834.
RAMON VINAY, 1912.

---

Friday **1**

ENGELBERT HUMPERDINCK, 1854.
GERTRUDE KAPPEL, 1884.
SEIJI OZAWA, 1935.

---

September

| S | M | T | W | T | F | S |
|---|---|---|---|---|---|---|
|   |   |   |   |   | 1 | 2 |
| 3 | 4 | 5 | 6 | 7 | 8 | 9 |
| 10 | 11 | 12 | 13 | 14 | 15 | 16 |
| 17 | 18 | 19 | 20 | 21 | 22 | 23 |
| 24 | 25 | 26 | 27 | 28 | 29 | 30 |

Saturday **2**

Sunday **3**

FRIEDRICH SCHORR, 1888.
SET SVANHOLM, 1904.

# September

Monday                                                            4

Tuesday                                                           5

GIACOMO MEYERBEER, 1791.
META SEINEMEYER, 1895.
KARITA MATTILA, 1960.

Wednesday                                                         6

DAVID STIVENDER, 1933.

Thursday                                                          7

JOAN CROSS, 1900.

Friday                                                            8

ANTONIN DVORÁK, 1841.
NINON VALLIN, 1886.
CHRISTOPH VON DOHNÁNYI, 1929.

Saturday                        9          Sunday               10

CHRISTOPHER HOGWOOD, 1941.
THOMAS ALLEN, 1944.

---

1966: THE NEW MET
AUDITORIUM

When the new theater
finally opened on Septem-
ber 16, 1966, it offered
splendors we now take for
granted: a stately, red-car-
peted grand staircase, a
series of beautiful star-
burst chandeliers (the gift
of the Austrian govern-
ment) and two magnificent
Marc Chagall murals. For
opening night Bing com-
missioned Samuel Barber
to compose a new opera,
*Antony and Cleopatra*,
which starred Leontyne
Price as the Queen of the
Nile. Franco Zeffirelli
designed and directed a
production that was suit-
ably grand for the opening
of an opera house but a bit
too grand for Barber's
opera. The hit of the
evening was the theater
itself.

Photograph courtesy of
*Opera News*

October

| S | M | T | W | T | F | S |
|---|---|---|---|---|---|---|
| 1 | 2 | 3 | 4 | 5 | 6 | 7 |
| 8 | 9 | 10 | 11 | 12 | 13 | 14 |
| 15 | 16 | 17 | 18 | 19 | 20 | 21 |
| 22 | 23 | 24 | 25 | 26 | 27 | 28 |
| 29 | 30 | 31 | | | | |

# September

1966: LEONIE
RYSANEK AND JAMES
KING IN *DIE FRAU
OHNE SCHATTEN*

Because the stage of the
new house was so much
larger than that of the old
Met, Bing knew that most
of the old productions
would have to be replaced
eventually. For the first
season he planned an
ambitious schedule of nine
new productions, including
two world premieres and
one opera never before
given by the Met. This last
was Richard Strauss's *Die
Frau ohne Schatten,* which
received a sensational production directed by
Nathaniel Merrill and
designed by Robert
O'Hearn. The cast, led by
Leonie Rysanek, Christa
Ludwig, Irene Dalis, James
King and Walter Berry,
was conducted by Karl
Böhm.

Photography courtesy of
the Education Department,
Metropolitan Opera Guild
© 1999 Metropolitan Opera
Guild, Inc.

**Monday** 11

**Tuesday** 12

MARIANNE BRANDT, 1842.
TATIANA TROYANOS, 1938.

**Wednesday** 13

FULL MOON

ARNOLD SCHOENBERG, 1874.
NICOLAI GHIAUROV, 1929.
ARLEEN AUGER, 1939.

**Thursday** 14

LUIGI CHERUBINI, 1760.

**Friday** 15

BRUNO WALTER, 1876.
HILDE GUEDEN, 1917.
JESSYE NORMAN, 1945.

**Saturday** 16

THE NEW MET OPENS WITH THE WORLD
PREMIERE OF BARBER'S *ANTONY AND
CLEOPATRA,* 1966.

**Sunday** 17

PETER ALLEN, 1920.

### October

| S | M | T | W | T | F | S |
|---|---|---|---|---|---|---|
| 1 | 2 | 3 | 4 | 5 | 6 | 7 |
| 8 | 9 | 10 | 11 | 12 | 13 | 14 |
| 15 | 16 | 17 | 18 | 19 | 20 | 21 |
| 22 | 23 | 24 | 25 | 26 | 27 | 28 |
| 29 | 30 | 31 | | | | |

# September

## Monday 18

1967: JON VICKERS IN
*PETER GRIMES*

Benjamin Britten's masterwork had been staged by
the Met in 1948 but did
not really find an audience
until the opening of a new
production during the
Met's first season in the
new theater. Theater director Tyrone Guthrie was in
charge, sets were by Tanya
Moiseiwitsch and the
orchestra led by Colin
Davis. The strong ensem-
ble cast included Lucine
Amara, Geraint Evans and
Jean Madeira. But above
all there was Jon Vickers's
towering performance in
the title role, a portrayal
Met audiences were lucky
enough to see thirty-eight
times over the next sixteen
years.

Photograph courtesy of
the Education Department,
Metropolitan Opera Guild
© 1999 Metropolitan Opera
Guild, Inc.

## Tuesday 19

BLANCHE THEBOM, 1918.

## Wednesday 20

## Thursday 21

SHIRLEY VERRETT MAKES HER MET DEBUT AS CARMEN, 1968.

## Friday 22

FIRST DAY OF AUTUMN

HERBERT JANSSEN, 1892.
ELISABETH RETHBERG, 1894.
ANNA TOMOWA-SINTOW, 1941.

## Saturday 23

JARMILA NOVOTNÁ, 1907.

## Sunday 24

KARIN BRANZELL, 1891.
ETTORE BASTIANINI, 1922.
CORNELL MACNEIL, 1922.
ALFREDO KRAUS, 1927.

### October

| S | M | T | W | T | F | S |
|---|---|---|---|---|---|---|
| 1 | 2 | 3 | 4 | 5 | 6 | 7 |
| 8 | 9 | 10 | 11 | 12 | 13 | 14 |
| 15 | 16 | 17 | 18 | 19 | 20 | 21 |
| 22 | 23 | 24 | 25 | 26 | 27 | 28 |
| 29 | 30 | 31 | | | | |

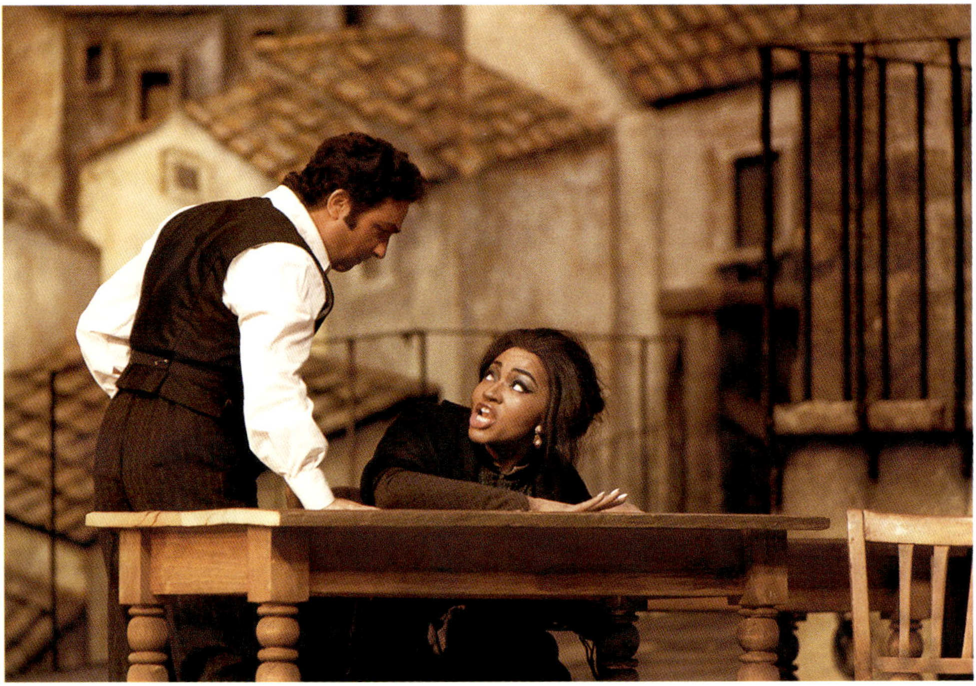

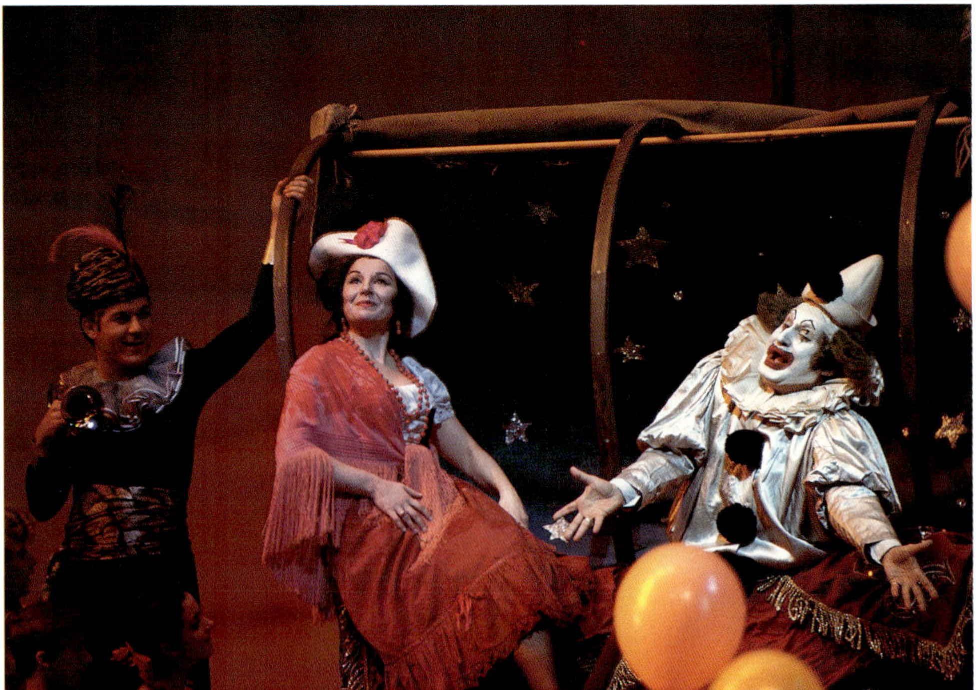

1970: *CAVALLERIA RUSTICANA AND PAGLIACCI*

Franco Zeffirelli designed and staged new productions of Mascagni's *Cavalleria Rusticana* and Leoncavallo's *Pagliacci* in 1970, both of which were well received by audiences and critics alike. (Rejecting the word "revival" in his review, Irving Kolodin wrote, ". . . what is happening at the Metropolitan may better be characterized as a rebirth, a renaissance, also a rejuvenation.") The Mascagni opera boasted a cast led by Grace Bumbry and Franco Corelli and was conducted by Leonard Bernstein. In the second half of the bill, Richard Tucker sang Canio to the Nedda of Lucine Amara (who was replacing an ailing Teresa Stratas) and the Tonio of Sherrill Milnes; they were conducted by Fausto Cleva.

Photos courtesy of the Education Department, Metropolitan Opera Guild © 1999 Metropolitan Opera Guild, Inc.

**Monday** 25

DMITRI SHOSTAKOVICH, 1906.
COLIN DAVIS, 1927.

**Tuesday** 26

GEORGE GERSHWIN, 1898.
FRITZ WUNDERLICH, 1930.
GARY LAKES, 1950.

**Wednesday** 27

JOSEPHINE BARSTOW, 1940.

**Thursday** 28

PLÁCIDO DOMINGO MAKES HIS MET DEBUT IN *ADRIANA LECOUVREUR*, 1968.

**Friday** 29

RICHARD BONYNGE, 1930.

**Saturday** 30

**Sunday** 1

ROSH HASHANAH

### October

| S | M | T | W | T | F | S |
|---|---|---|---|---|---|---|
| 1 | 2 | 3 | 4 | 5 | 6 | 7 |
| 8 | 9 | 10 | 11 | 12 | 13 | 14 |
| 15 | 16 | 17 | 18 | 19 | 20 | 21 |
| 22 | 23 | 24 | 25 | 26 | 27 | 28 |
| 29 | 30 | 31 | | | | |

# October

Monday    2

Tuesday    3

MING CHO LEE, 1930.
RUGGERO RAIMONDI, 1941.

Wednesday    4

GÖTA LJUNGBERG, 1893.
MARGHERITA GRANDI, 1894.

Thursday    5

Friday    6

JENNY LIND, 1820.
MARIA JERITZA, 1887.

Saturday    7    Sunday    8

CHARLES DUTOIT, 1936.
GRACE BUMBRY MAKES HER MET DEBUT AS
PRINCESS EBOLI, 1965.

---

1970/1985: FRANCO ZEFFIRELLI DESIGNS FOR *PAGLIACCI* AND *TOSCA*

Franco Zeffirelli, one of the most popular producers of opera in the second half of this century, has endured critical brickbats to see his productions live long lives at the Met. To date, he has directed and designed sets for a dozen Met productions, and for the first four he designed the costumes as well. His detractors call his recent work overblown, complaining that his singers are often lost on his massive sets. But most of his productions have triumphantly stood the test of time—his 1963 *Falstaff* is the only production from the old Met still in use.

Photographs courtesy of *Opera News*

---

November

| S | M | T | W | T | F | S |
|---|---|---|---|---|---|---|
| | | | 1 | 2 | 3 | 4 |
| 5 | 6 | 7 | 8 | 9 | 10 | 11 |
| 12 | 13 | 14 | 15 | 16 | 17 | 18 |
| 19 | 20 | 21 | 22 | 23 | 24 | 25 |
| 26 | 27 | 28 | 29 | 30 | | |

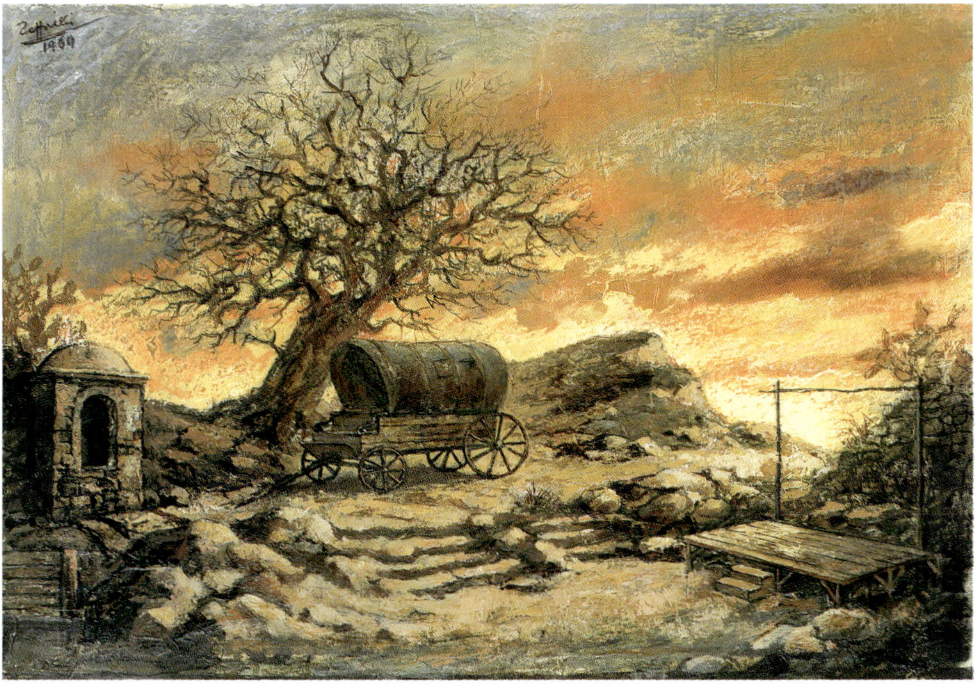

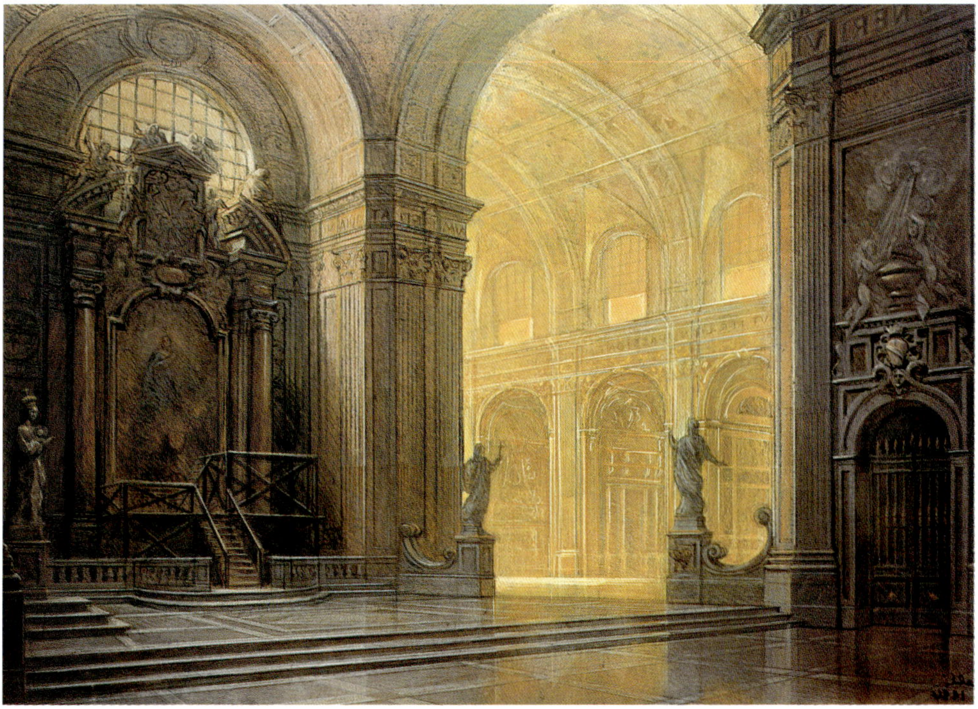

# October

## 1971: BIRGIT NILSSON AND JESS THOMAS IN *TRISTAN UND ISOLDE*

Birgit Nilsson's 1959 Met debut as Isolde in a new production was newsworthy enough to be reported on the front page of the *New York Times*, and twelve years later the Met mounted yet another new production of the work for her. August Everding's staging and Günther Schneider-Siemssen's designs made ample use of projections, allowing the naturalistically depicted "real world" to disappear when Tristan and Isolde drink their love potion, as well as the Met's extraordinary stage machinery, which lifted the lovers high in the air as they sang their second act love duet. Everding later recalled that when the production was staged, ". . . it was a time of drugs, of getting away, of escaping, of the first man in space, of acid trips, of astrology." In addition to Miss Nilsson, the first cast boasted Jess Thomas as Tristan, Mignon Dunn as Brangäne, Thomas Stewart as Kurwenal and John Macurdy as King Marke, conducted by Erich Leinsdorf.

Photograph © Beth Bergman 1999

### November

| S | M | T | W | T | F | S |
|---|---|---|---|---|---|---|
| | | | | 1 | 2 | 3 | 4 |
| 5 | 6 | 7 | 8 | 9 | 10 | 11 |
| 12 | 13 | 14 | 15 | 16 | 17 | 18 |
| 19 | 20 | 21 | 22 | 23 | 24 | 25 |
| 26 | 27 | 28 | 29 | 30 | | |

Monday 9

YOM KIPPUR
COLUMBUS DAY (US)
THANKSGIVING DAY (CANADA)
CAMILLE SAINT-SAËNS, 1835.
IRMGARD SEEFRIED, 1919.

Tuesday 10

GIUSEPPE VERDI, 1813.
LEYLA GENCER, 1924.

Wednesday 11

FERNANDO DE LUCIA, 1860.

Thursday 12

LUCIANO PAVAROTTI, 1935

Friday 13

FULL MOON
LEONA MITCHELL, 1949.
ELISABETH SCHWARZKOPF MAKES HER MET DEBUT IN *DER ROSENKAVALIER*, 1964, AND RENATA SCOTTO BOWS AS CIO-CIO-SAN, 1965.

Saturday 14

Sunday 15

BRUNA CASTAGNA, 1905.
SELMA KURZ, 1874.

# October

Monday                                                    16

DMITRI HVOROSTOVSKY, 1962.

Tuesday                                                   17

GIOVANNI MARIO, 1810.

Wednesday                                                 18

THE MET GIVES THE U.S. PREMIERE OF BENJAMIN BRITTEN'S *DEATH IN VENICE*. 1974.

Thursday                                                  19

ERNA BERGER, 1900.
BENITA VALENTE, 1934.

Friday                                                    20

Saturday                  21    Sunday                    22

GEORG SOLTI, 1912.                 GIOVANNI MARTINELLI, 1885.
JOHN ALEXANDER, 1923.              THE METROPOLITAN OPERA HOUSE
                                   OPENS WITH GOUNOD'S *FAUST*. 1883.

1972: JOAN SUTHERLAND AND LUCIANO PAVAROTTI IN *LA FILLE DU RÉGIMENT*

Two of the most significant singers of the twentieth century—one an established star and the other poised for stardom—joined forces for a new production of Donizetti's bubbly *La Fille du Régiment* in 1972, and lovers of bel canto were in ecstasy. Sutherland had made a sensational Met debut as Lucia di Lammermoor some ten years earlier, but this new production gave her a chance to prove her previously unsuspected comic skills. Her tenor cohort, whose career she had encouraged in an earlier tour of her native Australia, had had an inauspicious Met debut in 1968 but made headlines in *Fille du Régiment* primarily for the ease with which he dispensed high Cs. Staged by Sandro Sequi and conducted by Richard Bonynge, the cast also included Fernando Corena, Regina Resnik, and in a comic turn, Ljuba Welitsch.

### November

| S | M | T | W | T | F | S |
|---|---|---|---|---|---|---|
|   |   |   | 1 | 2 | 3 | 4 |
| 5 | 6 | 7 | 8 | 9 | 10 | 11 |
| 12 | 13 | 14 | 15 | 16 | 17 | 18 |
| 19 | 20 | 21 | 22 | 23 | 24 | 25 |
| 26 | 27 | 28 | 29 | 30 |   |   |

## 1972: THE BING FAREWELL

After twenty-two years as general manager of the Met, Rudolf Bing stepped down, and on April 22, 1972, he was honored with a gala performance sponsored by the Metropolitan Opera Guild. Many of the great artists who had appeared during his administration paid tribute to him, including Anna Moffo (above left) and Regina Resnik (above right), who dressed as Prince Orlofsky to sing a parody called "Chacon à Bing's Gout." While members of the company looked on, the honoree was presented with gold-lettered testimonial. An hour of the event was televised.

Photographs © Beth Bergman 1999

---

**Monday** 23

DENISE DUVAL, 1921.

---

**Tuesday** 24

SENA JURINAC, 1921.
TITO GOBBI, 1913.
CHERYL STUDER, 1955.

---

**Wednesday** 25

JOHANN STRAUSS, JR. 1825.
GEORGES BIZET, 1838.
FLORENCE EASTON, 1882.
GALINA VISHNEVSKAYA, 1926.

---

**Thursday** 26

GIUDITTA PASTA, 1797.
TIANA LEMNITZ, 1897.

---

**Friday** 27

---

### November

| S | M | T | W | T | F | S |
|---|---|---|---|---|---|---|
|   |   |   | 1 | 2 | 3 | 4 |
| 5 | 6 | 7 | 8 | 9 | 10 | 11 |
| 12 | 13 | 14 | 15 | 16 | 17 | 18 |
| 19 | 20 | 21 | 22 | 23 | 24 | 25 |
| 26 | 27 | 28 | 29 | 30 |   |   |

**Saturday** 28

TERESA STRATAS MAKES HER MET DEBUT AS POUSETTE IN *MANON*, 1959.

**Sunday** 29

JON VICKERS, 1926
MARIA CALLAS MAKES HER DEBUT AT *NORMA*, 1956

# October/November

**Monday** 30

**Tuesday** 31

HALLOWEEN

AUGUST EVERDING, 1928.
PETER WEXLER, 1936.

**Wednesday** 1

EMMA ALBANI, 1847.
VICTORIA DE LOS ANGELES, 1923.
EZIO PINZA MAKES HIS DEBUT IN *LA VESTALE*. 1926,
AND NICOLAI GEDDA HAS HIS IN *FAUST*. 1957.

**Thursday** 2

GIUSEPPE SINOPOLI, 1946.

**Friday** 3

VINCENZO BELLINI, 1801.

**Saturday** 4

LUCIENNE BRÉVAL, 1869.

**Sunday** 5

ANTHONY ROLFE JOHNSON, 1940

---

### 1972: MARILYN HORNE IN *CARMEN*

Rudolf Bing's successor, the Swedish director and producer Göran Gentele, had already planned many projects for the Met when he was killed in an automobile accident before his first season had begun, and Schuyler G. Chapin was appointed acting general manager (a year later he was given the full title). Opening night of Gentele's first season was to be his staging of *Carmen*, and the show went on, supervised by Bodo Igesz, designed by Josef Svoboda and conducted by Leonard Bernstein. Marilyn Horne was a spirited Carmen, with James McCracken, Adriana Maliponte and Tom Krause in the other leading roles.

### November

| S | M | T | W | T | F | S |
|---|---|---|---|---|---|---|
| | | | 1 | 2 | 3 | 4 |
| 5 | 6 | 7 | 8 | 9 | 10 | 11 |
| 12 | 13 | 14 | 15 | 16 | 17 | 18 |
| 19 | 20 | 21 | 22 | 23 | 24 | 25 |
| 26 | 27 | 28 | 29 | 30 | | |

# November

1977: RENATA SCOTTO
AND LUCIANO
PAVAROTTI IN *LA
BOHÈME*

Beginning with the
1975–76 season, the
Met was administered by
a troika consisting of
Anthony A. Bliss as execu-
tive director, John Dexter
as director of production
and James Levine as music
director. One of this team's
major achievements was
the inauguration of regular
Met performances on tele-
vision. While experiments
in the medium had been
made as early as 1940,
none seemed to work until
March 15, 1977, when
about four million homes
tuned in to see the Met at
its best: Renata Scotto,
Luciano Pavarotti, Maralin
Niska and Ingvar Wixell
in *La Bohème,* conducted by
James Levine. From that
time on, several operas
have been televised each
year from the Met stage.

Photograph courtesy of
the Education Department,
Metropolitan Opera Guild
© 1999 Metropolitan Opera
Guild, Inc.

## Monday
### 6

THE MET GIVES THE U.S. PREMIERE OF STRAUSS' *DIE AEGYPTISCHE HELENA.* 1928.

## Tuesday
### 7

ELECTION DAY (US)

JOAN SUTHERLAND, 1926.
GWYNETH JONES, 1936.

## Wednesday
### 8

LOUISE KIRKBY LUNN, 1873.
JEROME HINES, 1921.

## Thursday
### 9

PIERO CAPPUCCILLI, 1929.
NEW YORK CITY BLACKOUT CANCELS A PERFORMANCE OF *IL TROVATORE.* 1965.

## Friday
### 10

## Saturday
### 11

VETERANS DAY (US)

FULL MOON

ARMISTICE COINCIDES WITH THE MET 1918
OPENING NIGHT—CARUSO AND HOMER IN
*SAMSON ET DALILA.*

## Sunday
### 12

ALEXANDER BORODIN, 1833.
LUCIA POPP, 1939.

| December | | | | | | |
|---|---|---|---|---|---|---|
| S | M | T | W | T | F | S |
| | | | | | 1 | 2 |
| 3 | 4 | 5 | 6 | 7 | 8 | 9 |
| 10 | 11 | 12 | 13 | 14 | 15 | 16 |
| 17 | 18 | 19 | 20 | 21 | 22 | 23 |
| 24 | 25 | 26 | 27 | 28 | 29 | 30 |
| 31 | | | | | | |

# November

Monday    13

REMEMBRANCE DAY OBSERVED (CANADA)

GEORGE LONDON HAS HIS MET DEBUT AS AMONASRO, 1951.

Tuesday    14

LEONIE RYSANEK, 1926.

Wednesday    15

ROSA PONSELLE MAKES HER MET DEBUT IN THE U.S. PREMIERE OF
VERDI'S *LA FORZA DEL DESTINO*. 1918.

Thursday    16

LAWRENCE TIBBETT, 1896.
THE MET PRESENTS THE U.S. PREMIERE OF PUCCINI'S LAST OPERA, *TURANDOT*. 1926.

Friday    17

CHARLES MACKERRAS, 1925.

Saturday    18      Sunday    19

CARL MARIA VON WEBER, 1786.
AMELITA GALLI-CURCI, 1882.
MARIA IVOGÜN, 1891.

AGNES BALTSA, 1944.
MARIA JERITZA MAKES HER MET DEBUT
IN THE U.S. PREMIERE OF
KORNGOLD'S *DIE TOTE STADT*. 1921.

---

1979: PLÁCIDO
DOMINGO AND
SHERRILL MILNES
IN *OTELLO*

While not the first Met
opening night to be tele-
cast—early Met telecasts
included opening nights in
1948, 1949 and 1950—
the 1979 opening night
*Otello* was the first to be
seen by a national audience
on PBS. It also offered the
first Met Otello of Plácido
Domingo, who has become
the Otello of his genera-
tion, repeating his characterization in many subse-
quent Met seasons as well
as on film. The cast also
included Gilda Cruz-Romo
as Desdemona and Sherrill
Milnes as Iago, and was
conducted by James
Levine. Opening night at
the Met has been telecast
only three times since—in
1991, 1994 and 1998.

Photograph © Beth Bergman
1999

---

December

| S | M | T | W | T | F | S |
|---|---|---|---|---|---|---|
|   |   |   |   |   | 1 | 2 |
| 3 | 4 | 5 | 6 | 7 | 8 | 9 |
| 10 | 11 | 12 | 13 | 14 | 15 | 16 |
| 17 | 18 | 19 | 20 | 21 | 22 | 23 |
| 24 | 25 | 26 | 27 | 28 | 29 | 30 |
| 31 |   |   |   |   |   |   |

# November

1981: TERESA STRATAS
AND JOSÉ CARRERAS
IN *LA BOHÈME*

Franco Zeffirelli had been
away from the Met for
nearly ten years when his
new production of *La
Bohème* opened on Decem-
ber 14, 1981. An immedi-
ate hit with Met audiences
(as usual, critics were
divided), the production
has been seen nearly every
season since and shows no
signs of losing its popu-
larity. Zeffirelli told a
writer that his goal was to
"bring out the fragility of
the Bohemian group as
against the large, gray
French capital. . . . I want
to underline the helpless-
ness and humanity of those
nice young people lost in
that large city." Teresa
Stratas and José Carreras
were the production's
first Mimì and Rodolfo,
with Renata Scotto as
Musetta, Richard Stilwell
as Marcello and James
Morris as Colline. James
Levine conducted.

Photograph by William
Harris, courtesy of the
Education Department,
Metropolitan Opera Guild
© 1999 Metropolitan Opera
Guild, Inc.

**Monday** 20

RENÉ KOLLO, 1937.
BARBARA HENDRICKS, 1948.

**Tuesday** 21

**Wednesday** 22

BENJAMIN BRITTEN, 1913.
SUMI JO, 1962.
RISË STEVENS MAKES HER MET DEBUT IN *DER ROSENKAVALIER*. 1938.

**Thursday** 23

THANKSGIVING (US)
ENRICO CARUSO MAKES HIS MET DEBUT IN *RIGOLETTO*. 1903,
AND LUCIANO PAVAROTTI HAS HIS DEBUT IN *LA BOHÈME*. 1968.

**Friday** 24

LILLI LEHMANN, 1848.

**Saturday** 25

VIRGIL THOMSON, 1896.
HÅKAN HAGEGÅRD, 1945.
LILLI LEHMANN HAS HER MET DEBUT
IN A GERMAN-LANGUAGE *CARMEN*. 1885.

**Sunday** 26

GERALDINE FARRAR MAKES HER MET
DEBUT AS GOUNOD'S JULIETTE, 1906,
AND JOAN SUTHERLAND HAS HER DEBUT
AS LUCIA, 1961.

| December | | | | | | |
|---|---|---|---|---|---|---|
| S | M | T | W | T | F | S |
| | | | | | 1 | 2 |
| 3 | 4 | 5 | 6 | 7 | 8 | 9 |
| 10 | 11 | 12 | 13 | 14 | 15 | 16 |
| 17 | 18 | 19 | 20 | 21 | 22 | 23 |
| 24 | 25 | 26 | 27 | 28 | 29 | 30 |
| 31 | | | | | | |

# November/December

Monday

## 27

THE MET RE-OPENS HAVING BEEN REBUILT AFTER ITS FIRE, 1893.

Tuesday

## 28

SUZANNE ADAMS, 1872.
ROSE BAMPTON, 1909.
HELEN JEPSON, 1904.

Wednesday

## 29

GAETANO DONIZETTI, 1797.
JAN PEERCE BOWS AS *LA TRAVIATA'S* ALFREDO, 1941.

Thursday

## 30

Friday

## 1

THE MET PRESENTS THE U.S. PREMIERE OF WAGNER'S *TRISTAN UND ISOLDE*, 1886.
DOROTHY KIRSTEN MAKES HER MET DEBUT AS MIMÌ, 1945.

Saturday

## 2

Sunday

## 3

PAUL ALTHOUSE, 1889.
MARIA CALLAS, 1923.
IRINA ARKHIPOVA, 1925.

TANYA MOISEIWITSCH, 1913.
PHYLLIS CURTIN, 1921.

## 1983: THE CENTENNIAL GALA

On October 22, 1993, the Met celebrated its one hundredth birthday with a two-part, day-long gala concert, televised live on PBS. Nearly ninety important singers joined the Metropolitan Opera Chorus and Orchestra in arias and ensembles, and the conductors included James Levine, Leonard Bernstein and Richard Bonynge. Toward the end of the evening program, a group of honored guests—great artists of the past—was assembled on the stage, including Risë Stevens, Zinka Milanov, Dorothy Kirsten, Eleanor Steber, Bidù Sayão and Jarmila Novotna. And for the grand finale, the entire company gathered onstage to sing "Happy Birthday." Flanking James Levine at the final curtain were Roberta Peters and Birgit Nilsson.

Photograph © Beth Bergman 1999

| December | | | | | | |
|---|---|---|---|---|---|---|
| S | M | T | W | T | F | S |
| | | | | | 1 | 2 |
| 3 | 4 | 5 | 6 | 7 | 8 | 9 |
| 10 | 11 | 12 | 13 | 14 | 15 | 16 |
| 17 | 18 | 19 | 20 | 21 | 22 | 23 |
| 24 | 25 | 26 | 27 | 28 | 29 | 30 |
| 31 | | | | | | |

# December

## 1985: SIMON ESTES AND GRACE BUMBRY IN *PORGY AND BESS*

Since its Broadway opening in 1935, *Porgy and Bess* has uncomfortably straddled the worlds of opera and musical comedy. Intended as an opera by its creators, George and Ira Gershwin and DuBose Heyward, the work's Broadway premiere was covered by both theatrical and musical press. (Several of the music critics refused to take the piece seriously.) Later Broadway revivals replaced Gershwin's sung recitative with spoken dialogue, but in the 1970s Houston Grand Opera mounted a successful production that adhered more closely to Gershwin's concept, and a Met production finally opened on February 6, 1985. James Levine conducted a cast that included Simon Estes, Grace Bumbry, Charles Williams, Gregg Baker, Florence Quivar and Myra Merritt.

Photograph by William Harris, courtesy of the Education Department, Metropolitan Opera Guild © 1999 Metropolitan Opera Guild, Inc.

### Monday · 4

LUCREZIA BORI, 1887.
YVONNE MINTON, 1938.
CLAUDIA MUZIO MAKES HER MET DEBUT AS TOSCA, 1916.

### Tuesday · 5

GRACE MOORE, 1898.
JOSÉ CARRERAS, 1946.

### Wednesday · 6

LUIGI LABLACHE, 1794.
ASTRID VARNEY MAKES HER MET DEBUT IN *DIE WALKÜRE*, 1941,
AND REGINA RESNIK HAS HERS IN *IL TROVATORE*, 1944.

### Thursday · 7

PIETRO MASCAGNI, 1863.
SYBIL SANDERSON, 1865.
ELISABETH HÖNGEN, 1906.
TEXACO BEGINS ITS SPONSORSHIP OF THE MET SATURDAY BROADCASTS, 1940.

### Friday · 8

TULLIO SERAFIN, 1878.

### Saturday · 9

CONCHITA SUPERVIA, 1895.
ELISABETH SCHWARZKOPF, 1915.

### Sunday · 10

HUMAN RIGHTS DAY

THE MET PRESENTS THE WORLD PREMIERE OF PUCCINI'S *LA FANCIULLA DEL WEST*, 1910.

### January 2001

| S | M | T | W | T | F | S |
|---|---|---|---|---|---|---|
|   | 1 | 2 | 3 | 4 | 5 | 6 |
| 7 | 8 | 9 | 10 | 11 | 12 | 13 |
| 14 | 15 | 16 | 17 | 18 | 19 | 20 |
| 21 | 22 | 23 | 24 | 25 | 26 | 27 |
| 28 | 29 | 30 | 31 |   |   |   |

# December

FULL MOON

HECTOR BERLIOZ, 1803.
GIACOMO LAURI-VOLPI, 1892.

Tuesday    12

LUDWIG SUTHAUS, 1906.

Wednesday    13

ELEANOR ROBSON BELMONT, FOUNDER OF THE METROPOLITAN OPERA GUILD, 1878.
ANTONIO PAPPANO, 1959.

Thursday    14

GEORGES THILL, 1897.
RICHARD CASSILLY, 1927.
THE MET PRESENTS THE WORLD PREMIERE OF PUCCINI'S *IL TRITTICO*, 1918.

Friday    15

RAINA KABAIVANSKA, 1934.
ROBERT MERRILL MAKES HIS MET DEBUT AS THE ELDER GERMONT, 1945.

Saturday    16      Sunday    17

JAMES MCCRACKEN, 1926.

LUDWIG VAN BEETHOVEN, 1770.
ZINKA MILANOW MAKES HER MET DEBUT
IN *IL TROVATORE*, 1937.

---

1991: *THE GHOSTS OF VERSAILLES*

On December 19, 1991, the Met gave the world premiere of *The Ghosts of Versailles*, with music by John Corigliano and a libretto by William M. Hoffman. It was the first world premiere to be presented by the Met in twenty-five years, and the opera became the hottest ticket of the season. The complicated plot imagined the ghost of Beaumarchais creating a sequel to his Figaro story in an attempt to amuse the ghost of Marie Antoinette and perhaps to change the course of history. The large cast was headed by Teresa Stratas, Marilyn Horne, Håkan Hagegård, Graham Clark, Gino Quilico, and in this scene, Tracy Dahl, Neil Rosenshein, Judith Cristin, Renée Fleming and Peter Kazaras. The production, conducted by James Levine, was later telecast.

Photograph by William Harris, courtesy of the Education Department, Metropolitan Opera Guild © 1999 Metropolitan Opera Guild, Inc.

| January 2001 | | | | | | |
|---|---|---|---|---|---|---|
| S | M | T | W | T | F | S |
| | 1 | 2 | 3 | 4 | 5 | 6 |
| 7 | 8 | 9 | 10 | 11 | 12 | 13 |
| 14 | 15 | 16 | 17 | 18 | 19 | 20 |
| 21 | 22 | 23 | 24 | 25 | 26 | 27 |
| 28 | 29 | 30 | 31 | | | |

# December

1996: THE JAMES
LEVINE TWENTY-
FIFTH ANNIVERSARY
GALA

On April 27, 1996, most
of the opera world gath-
ered on the Met stage to
celebrate the twenty-fifth
anniversary of James
Levine's Metropolitan
Opera debut. In that quar-
ter of a century, Maestro
Levine not only progressed
from principal conductor
to music director to artistic
director of the company,
but took the lead in
broadening the Met's
repertory, all the while
raising the playing of the
Met Orchestra to the point
where it is now considered
a major American orches-
tra. (He has also conducted
more performances than
anyone else in Met history.)
A roster of extraordinary
singers gathered to help
celebrate Maestro Levine's
accomplishments; seen
here are Karita Mattila and
Håkan Hagegård (top left),
Bryn Terfel and Kiri Te
Kanawa (top right) and
Deborah Voigt and Plácido
Domingo (bottom). Mae-
stro Levine conducted the
entire concert, which was
telecast live.

Photographs © Beth
Bergman 1999

## January 2001

| S | M | T | W | T | F | S |
|---|---|---|---|---|---|---|
| | 1 | 2 | 3 | 4 | 5 | 6 |
| 7 | 8 | 9 | 10 | 11 | 12 | 13 |
| 14 | 15 | 16 | 17 | 18 | 19 | 20 |
| 21 | 22 | 23 | 24 | 25 | 26 | 27 |
| 28 | 29 | 30 | 31 | | | |

---

**Monday 18**

RITA STREICH, 1920.
BIRGIT NILSSON MAKES HER MET DEBUT AS ISOLDE, 1959.

---

**Tuesday 19**

MILKA TERNINA, 1863.
FRITZ REINER, 1888.
DUSOLINA GIANNINI, 1900.

---

**Wednesday 20**

---

**Thursday 21**

FIRST DAY OF WINTER
ZELIE DE LUSSAN, 1861.

---

**Friday 22**

HANUKKAH

EDOUARD DE RESZKE, 1853.
GIACOMO PUCCINI, 1858.
FERNANDO CORENA, 1916.
NADINE CONNER MAKES HER DEBUT AS PAMINA, 1941,
AND MONSERRAT CABALLÉ AND SHERRILL MILNES SHARE DEBUTS IN *FAUST*, 1965.

---

**Saturday 23**

EDITA GRUBEROVA, 1946.

**Sunday 24**

ADAMO DIDUR, 1874.
TERESA STICH-RANDALL, 1927.

# December

## Monday — 25

CHRISTMAS

GIUSEPPE DE LUCA, 1876.
GLADYS SWARTHOUT, 1900.
THE FIRST COMPLETE MET RADIO BROADCAST IS *HANSEL AND GRETEL*. 1931.

## Tuesday — 26

BOXING DAY (UK & CANADA)

THE MET EMBARKS ON ITS FIRST TOUR WITH A PERFORMANCE OF GOUNOD'S *FAUST*.
IN BOSTON, 1883.

## Wednesday — 27

## Thursday — 28

FRANCESCO TAMAGNO, 1850.
GERALDINE FARRAR SHARES THE MET STAGE WITH A FLOCK OF LIVE GEESE
IN THE WORLD PREMIERE OF *KÖNIGSKINDER* IN 1910.

## Friday — 29

## Saturday — 30

## Sunday — 31

JUNE ANDERSON, 1952.

---

**1998: CECILIA BARTOLI AND SUSANNE MENTZER IN *LE NOZZE DI FIGARO***

Since the 1990–91 season, the Met has been led by Joseph Volpe, who at the turn of the century will have been with the company nearly forty years. Under his leadership, the Met has enjoyed a decade of financial stability and artistic strength. Among the many successful new productions presented by the company in the last years of the twentieth century was this 1998 *Le Nozze di Figaro,* directed by Jonathan Miller and conducted by James Levine. In the cast were Renée Fleming, Cecilia Bartoli, Susanne Mentzer, Bryn Terfel and Dwayne Croft.

Photograph © Beth Bergman 1999

### January 2001

| S | M | T | W | T | F | S |
|---|---|---|---|---|---|---|
|   | 1 | 2 | 3 | 4 | 5 | 6 |
| 7 | 8 | 9 | 10 | 11 | 12 | 13 |
| 14 | 15 | 16 | 17 | 18 | 19 | 20 |
| 21 | 22 | 23 | 24 | 25 | 26 | 27 |
| 28 | 29 | 30 | 31 |   |   |   |

# January 2001

| | |
|---|---|
| Monday | 1 |

GUSTAV MAHLER MAKES HIS MET DEBUT AS CONDUCTOR OF *TRISTAN AND ISOLDE*. 1908.

| | |
|---|---|
| Tuesday | 2 |

TITO SCHIPA, 1888.
MICHAEL TIPPETT, 1905.

| | |
|---|---|
| Wednesday | 3 |

HENRIETTE SONTAG, 1806.
LILY PONS MAKES HER MET DEBUT AS LUCIA, 1931.

| | |
|---|---|
| Thursday | 4 |

GRACE BUMBRY, 1937.
THE MET PRESENTS THE U.S. PREMIERE OF WAGNER'S *DIE MEISTERSINGER*. 1886.

| | |
|---|---|
| Friday | 5 |

ALEXANDER KIPNIS MAKES HIS MET DEBUT IN A MATINEE *PARSIFAL*. 1940,
AND JARMILA NOVOTNÁ BOWS THE SAME EVENING AS MIMÌ.

| | | | |
|---|---|---|---|
| Saturday | 6 | Sunday | 7 |

MAFALDA FAVERO, 1903.

FRANCIS POULENC, 1899.
JOHN BROWNLEE, 1901.

February

| S | M | T | W | T | F | S |
|---|---|---|---|---|---|---|
| | | | | 1 | 2 | 3 |
| 4 | 5 | 6 | 7 | 8 | 9 | 10 |
| 11 | 12 | 13 | 14 | 15 | 16 | 17 |
| 18 | 19 | 20 | 21 | 22 | 23 | 24 |
| 25 | 26 | 27 | 28 | | | |

# Birthdays and Anniversaries

# 2000

## January
| S | M | T | W | T | F | S |
|---|---|---|---|---|---|---|
|   |   |   |   |   |   | 1 |
| 2 | 3 | 4 | 5 | 6 | 7 | 8 |
| 9 | 10 | 11 | 12 | 13 | 14 | 15 |
| 16 | 17 | 18 | 19 | 20 | 21 | 22 |
| 23 | 24 | 25 | 26 | 27 | 28 | 29 |
| 30 | 31 |   |   |   |   |   |

## February
| S | M | T | W | T | F | S |
|---|---|---|---|---|---|---|
|   |   | 1 | 2 | 3 | 4 | 5 |
| 6 | 7 | 8 | 9 | 10 | 11 | 12 |
| 13 | 14 | 15 | 16 | 17 | 18 | 19 |
| 20 | 21 | 22 | 23 | 24 | 25 | 26 |
| 27 | 28 | 29 |   |   |   |   |

## March
| S | M | T | W | T | F | S |
|---|---|---|---|---|---|---|
|   |   |   | 1 | 2 | 3 | 4 |
| 5 | 6 | 7 | 8 | 9 | 10 | 11 |
| 12 | 13 | 14 | 15 | 16 | 17 | 18 |
| 19 | 20 | 21 | 22 | 23 | 24 | 25 |
| 26 | 27 | 28 | 29 | 30 | 31 |   |

## April
| S | M | T | W | T | F | S |
|---|---|---|---|---|---|---|
|   |   |   |   |   |   | 1 |
| 2 | 3 | 4 | 5 | 6 | 7 | 8 |
| 9 | 10 | 11 | 12 | 13 | 14 | 15 |
| 16 | 17 | 18 | 19 | 20 | 21 | 22 |
| 23 | 24 | 25 | 26 | 27 | 28 | 29 |
| 30 |   |   |   |   |   |   |

## May
| S | M | T | W | T | F | S |
|---|---|---|---|---|---|---|
|   | 1 | 2 | 3 | 4 | 5 | 6 |
| 7 | 8 | 9 | 10 | 11 | 12 | 13 |
| 14 | 15 | 16 | 17 | 18 | 19 | 20 |
| 21 | 22 | 23 | 24 | 25 | 26 | 27 |
| 28 | 29 | 30 | 31 |   |   |   |

## June
| S | M | T | W | T | F | S |
|---|---|---|---|---|---|---|
|   |   |   |   | 1 | 2 | 3 |
| 4 | 5 | 6 | 7 | 8 | 9 | 10 |
| 11 | 12 | 13 | 14 | 15 | 16 | 17 |
| 18 | 19 | 20 | 21 | 22 | 23 | 24 |
| 25 | 26 | 27 | 28 | 29 | 30 |   |

## July
| S | M | T | W | T | F | S |
|---|---|---|---|---|---|---|
|   |   |   |   |   |   | 1 |
| 2 | 3 | 4 | 5 | 6 | 7 | 8 |
| 9 | 10 | 11 | 12 | 13 | 14 | 15 |
| 16 | 17 | 18 | 19 | 20 | 21 | 22 |
| 23 | 24 | 25 | 26 | 27 | 28 | 29 |
| 30 | 31 |   |   |   |   |   |

## August
| S | M | T | W | T | F | S |
|---|---|---|---|---|---|---|
|   |   | 1 | 2 | 3 | 4 | 5 |
| 6 | 7 | 8 | 9 | 10 | 11 | 12 |
| 13 | 14 | 15 | 16 | 17 | 18 | 19 |
| 20 | 21 | 22 | 23 | 24 | 25 | 26 |
| 27 | 28 | 29 | 30 | 31 |   |   |

## September
| S | M | T | W | T | F | S |
|---|---|---|---|---|---|---|
|   |   |   |   |   | 1 | 2 |
| 3 | 4 | 5 | 6 | 7 | 8 | 9 |
| 10 | 11 | 12 | 13 | 14 | 15 | 16 |
| 17 | 18 | 19 | 20 | 21 | 22 | 23 |
| 24 | 25 | 26 | 27 | 28 | 29 | 30 |

## October
| S | M | T | W | T | F | S |
|---|---|---|---|---|---|---|
| 1 | 2 | 3 | 4 | 5 | 6 | 7 |
| 8 | 9 | 10 | 11 | 12 | 13 | 14 |
| 15 | 16 | 17 | 18 | 19 | 20 | 21 |
| 22 | 23 | 24 | 25 | 26 | 27 | 28 |
| 29 | 30 | 31 |   |   |   |   |

## November
| S | M | T | W | T | F | S |
|---|---|---|---|---|---|---|
|   |   |   | 1 | 2 | 3 | 4 |
| 5 | 6 | 7 | 8 | 9 | 10 | 11 |
| 12 | 13 | 14 | 15 | 16 | 17 | 18 |
| 19 | 20 | 21 | 22 | 23 | 24 | 25 |
| 26 | 27 | 28 | 29 | 30 |   |   |

## December
| S | M | T | W | T | F | S |
|---|---|---|---|---|---|---|
|   |   |   |   |   | 1 | 2 |
| 3 | 4 | 5 | 6 | 7 | 8 | 9 |
| 10 | 11 | 12 | 13 | 14 | 15 | 16 |
| 17 | 18 | 19 | 20 | 21 | 22 | 23 |
| 24 | 25 | 26 | 27 | 28 | 29 | 30 |
| 31 |   |   |   |   |   |   |

# 2001

## January
| S | M | T | W | T | F | S |
|---|---|---|---|---|---|---|
|   | 1 | 2 | 3 | 4 | 5 | 6 |
| 7 | 8 | 9 | 10 | 11 | 12 | 13 |
| 14 | 15 | 16 | 17 | 18 | 19 | 20 |
| 21 | 22 | 23 | 24 | 25 | 26 | 27 |
| 28 | 29 | 30 | 31 |   |   |   |

## February
| S | M | T | W | T | F | S |
|---|---|---|---|---|---|---|
|   |   |   |   | 1 | 2 | 3 |
| 4 | 5 | 6 | 7 | 8 | 9 | 10 |
| 11 | 12 | 13 | 14 | 15 | 16 | 17 |
| 18 | 19 | 20 | 21 | 22 | 23 | 24 |
| 25 | 26 | 27 | 28 |   |   |   |

## March
| S | M | T | W | T | F | S |
|---|---|---|---|---|---|---|
|   |   |   |   | 1 | 2 | 3 |
| 4 | 5 | 6 | 7 | 8 | 9 | 10 |
| 11 | 12 | 13 | 14 | 15 | 16 | 17 |
| 18 | 19 | 20 | 21 | 22 | 23 | 24 |
| 25 | 26 | 27 | 28 | 29 | 30 | 31 |

## April
| S | M | T | W | T | F | S |
|---|---|---|---|---|---|---|
| 1 | 2 | 3 | 4 | 5 | 6 | 7 |
| 8 | 9 | 10 | 11 | 12 | 13 | 14 |
| 15 | 16 | 17 | 18 | 19 | 20 | 21 |
| 22 | 23 | 24 | 25 | 26 | 27 | 28 |
| 29 | 30 |   |   |   |   |   |

## May
| S | M | T | W | T | F | S |
|---|---|---|---|---|---|---|
|   |   | 1 | 2 | 3 | 4 | 5 |
| 6 | 7 | 8 | 9 | 10 | 11 | 12 |
| 13 | 14 | 15 | 16 | 17 | 18 | 19 |
| 20 | 21 | 22 | 23 | 24 | 25 | 26 |
| 27 | 28 | 29 | 30 | 31 |   |   |

## June
| S | M | T | W | T | F | S |
|---|---|---|---|---|---|---|
|   |   |   |   |   | 1 | 2 |
| 3 | 4 | 5 | 6 | 7 | 8 | 9 |
| 10 | 11 | 12 | 13 | 14 | 15 | 16 |
| 17 | 18 | 19 | 20 | 21 | 22 | 23 |
| 24 | 25 | 26 | 27 | 28 | 29 | 30 |

## July
| S | M | T | W | T | F | S |
|---|---|---|---|---|---|---|
| 1 | 2 | 3 | 4 | 5 | 6 | 7 |
| 8 | 9 | 10 | 11 | 12 | 13 | 14 |
| 15 | 16 | 17 | 18 | 19 | 20 | 21 |
| 22 | 23 | 24 | 25 | 26 | 27 | 28 |
| 29 | 30 | 31 |   |   |   |   |

## August
| S | M | T | W | T | F | S |
|---|---|---|---|---|---|---|
|   |   |   | 1 | 2 | 3 | 4 |
| 5 | 6 | 7 | 8 | 9 | 10 | 11 |
| 12 | 13 | 14 | 15 | 16 | 17 | 18 |
| 19 | 20 | 21 | 22 | 23 | 24 | 25 |
| 26 | 27 | 28 | 29 | 30 | 31 |   |

## September
| S | M | T | W | T | F | S |
|---|---|---|---|---|---|---|
|   |   |   |   |   |   | 1 |
| 2 | 3 | 4 | 5 | 6 | 7 | 8 |
| 9 | 10 | 11 | 12 | 13 | 14 | 15 |
| 16 | 17 | 18 | 19 | 20 | 21 | 22 |
| 23 | 24 | 25 | 26 | 27 | 28 | 29 |
| 30 |   |   |   |   |   |   |

## October
| S | M | T | W | T | F | S |
|---|---|---|---|---|---|---|
|   | 1 | 2 | 3 | 4 | 5 | 6 |
| 7 | 8 | 9 | 10 | 11 | 12 | 13 |
| 14 | 15 | 16 | 17 | 18 | 19 | 20 |
| 21 | 22 | 23 | 24 | 25 | 26 | 27 |
| 28 | 29 | 30 | 31 |   |   |   |

## November
| S | M | T | W | T | F | S |
|---|---|---|---|---|---|---|
|   |   |   |   | 1 | 2 | 3 |
| 4 | 5 | 6 | 7 | 8 | 9 | 10 |
| 11 | 12 | 13 | 14 | 15 | 16 | 17 |
| 18 | 19 | 20 | 21 | 22 | 23 | 24 |
| 25 | 26 | 27 | 28 | 29 | 30 |   |

## December
| S | M | T | W | T | F | S |
|---|---|---|---|---|---|---|
|   |   |   |   |   |   | 1 |
| 2 | 3 | 4 | 5 | 6 | 7 | 8 |
| 9 | 10 | 11 | 12 | 13 | 14 | 15 |
| 16 | 17 | 18 | 19 | 20 | 21 | 22 |
| 23 | 24 | 25 | 26 | 27 | 28 | 29 |
| 30 | 31 |   |   |   |   |   |